THE
BASICS OF SYSTEMS
ANALYSIS AND
DESIGN FOR
INFORMATION
MANAGERS

THE
BASICS OF SYSTEMS ANALYSIS AND DESIGN FOR INFORMATION MANAGERS

JENNIFER E. ROWLEY

Senior Lecturer in Information Technology
Department of Library and Information Studies
Manchester Polytechnic

CLIVE BINGLEY  LONDON

© Jennifer E. Rowley 1990

Published by
Clive Bingley Limited
7 Ridgmount Street
London WC1E 7AE

First published 1990

British Library Cataloguing in Publication Data

Rowley, J. E. (Jennifer E)
 The basics of systems analysis and design for information managers.
 1. Information systems. Design
 I. Title
 302.2

 ISBN 0-85157-453-X

Photoset in 10/12pt Times by Library Association Publishing Ltd
Printed and bound in Great Britain by Bookcraft (Bath) Ltd

Contents

Acknowledgements

Many friends and colleagues have contributed to the creation of this book in a variety of ways, and I am grateful to them all.

My appreciation and presentation of the topics covered in this book have evolved over the past five years. During that time I have been teaching Systems Analysis and Design to students on the IT Cohort of the BA(Hons) Library and Information Studies courses at Manchester Polytechnic. Thanks are due to students who were members of the IT Cohort: to the first Cohort, including Tim, Sue, Carol, Laura, Voirrey, Sandra and Alison, who bore with me whilst I worked through the course for the first time; and to the second Cohort, Andy, Diane, Cathy, Jane, Libby, Tom, Jan, Martin, Julie, Sue, Tessa and Kay, who pushed me further in my appreciation of database management software than either they or I wanted to go! Lastly, none of this would have been possible without my colleague Tony Wood who not only conceived the IT Cohort, and attracted the funds that led to the Lectureship to which I was appointed at Manchester, but has also been the source of much useful information and inspiration. Thanks go to all of these, and to my family, particularly my husband, Peter, whose support has been so longstanding that it is difficult not to take it for granted.

Introduction

A library automation program should involve more complex, time-consuming and costly planning processes than other library programs because the impact of automation is so pervasive. In addition to significant budgetary implications, automation can require organisational changes, revisions in library policies and procedures, changes in the attributes of both staff and patrons, and complex contractual obligations. Automation is too complex and costly to undertake without first engaging in extensive investigation, discussion and decision making. (Boss, R. W., *The library manager's guide to automation*, 2nd ed., White Plains (NY), Knowledge Industry Publications, 1984.)

Computers have become well established as basic tools in library and information work. Falling hardware costs and the development of an extensive and reliable range of microcomputers have made computerization realistic for all information environments. Information professionals are likely to encounter a range of different kinds of computer systems, from library-housekeeping systems or database-management systems, through to word-processing systems and desktop-publishing systems. The investment in terms of cash and time, and the extent to which it is integral to the operation of a library or other organization, will vary but the need for a successful implementation is constant.

A decision to implement a computer system should only be made after a full consideration of the objectives of the scheme and all the methods of achieving them. In undertaking the implementation of a computer system, a systems-analysis-and-design methodology offers a well-tried framework. This acts as a control system which serves all parties involved in the systems exercise.

The adoption of a systems methodology offers a number of advantages.

Broadly, advantages for the manager include:

- Control over planning, since progress can be charted, and financial allocations can be predicted
- Standardized documentation which assists in communication throughout the systems planning and life
- Continuity provided as a contingency against key members of staff leaving the project.

Advantages to those carrying out the study include:

- Consideration of the requirements of any computer-based system requires the collection of a number of facts. A systematic approach helps to ensure completeness and facilitates collation.
- Having to produce details formally in writing encourages more careful consideration of each issue, which is more likely to lead to well-founded recommendations and conclusions.

The systems approach and systems methodologies are discussed more fully towards the end of the next chapter.

Systems analysis and design has become of central concern to the information professional, although the perspective of one information professional may differ from that of another.

This text, then, attempts to provide a basic introduction to systems analysis and design for the information professional. It should be particularly valuable to students who are commencing a course of study in this area, but is equally appropriate for the practising library and information professional who has some contact with computer systems (and that includes almost everybody!).

Naturally, awareness of techniques and methodologies is not sufficient. The next step is to apply these techniques to real systems.

There are many other ways that this book could have been written. Topics could have been included that have been omitted; different emphases could have been adopted. The author has wrestled for a long time with the most appropriate balance for this book, and has reluctantly concluded that perfection is an elusive dream. One major omission that has been necessary in the interests of brevity is details of specific computer systems, and their implementations. It has been necessary to deal in techniques, principles and generalities. Accounts of specific systems are, however, listed in the further reading at the end of each chapter.

In order to explain the perspective of this book further, it is necessary to refer to the role of the information professional in relation to computer systems. Information professionals may have a wide variety of roles in relation to computer systems. They may be any one of, or a combination of:

- System users, involved in the retrieval of data
- System users, involved in maintaining a database
- System managers, responsible for the overall management and control of the system
- System analysts, involved in the specification of systems requirements for a new and improved system
- System designers, involved in the design of the human – computer interface, and database design for a system
- System implementers, involved in the implementation of systems
- System suppliers, involved in the marketing of systems.

The information professional is not likely to take responsibility for a large mainframe- or mini-based installation serving an organization across many functions, but should make a contribution to the implementation of such a system and needs to understand the systems-analysis-and-design process. On the other hand, the information professional may be completely responsible for the implementation of a large library-housekeeping system, or a smaller microcomputer system for any one of a number of functions from word processing, and financial management to desktop publishing. Also, an information professional may be employed by systems or software suppliers in various functions such as marketing, education and user support.

This book, then, advocates the adaption of a systems approach in the selection, design and implementation of computer systems. Its primary purpose is to introduce the key concepts of systems analysis and design. Although the computer scientist or systems analyst may benefit from the explanations offered of some of these techniques, the book is not addressed primarily to the computer professional. It aims to introduce the information professional to the range of techniques that constitute the discipline of systems analysis and design. It is difficult to be comprehensive in such a short text, so there are inevitable omissions. It is hoped that this book provides a straightforward framework from which a more complete study of specific aspects of the field may be embarked upon, as required.

The structure of this book

Chapter One starts by offering some basic definitions and by establishing the context in which a systems-analysis-and-design exercise might be performed. It then proceeds to identify the main stages in a systems-analysis-and-design exercise and to explain the unique contribution of each of the stages. In doing this, Chapter One provides the framework for the other chapters of the book. The later chapters take the opportunity to focus on specific aspects of the systems-analysis-and-design process. Their content does not always reflect the sequence of a systems-analysis-and-design exercise, although, in general the data-collection and organization activities described in Chapter Two are likely to take place before the design activities of Chapters Three and Four, and implementation, the subject of Chapter Five, is likely to be the last stage of the project. On the other hand it would be extremely unwise to leave consideration of issues such as training and security, which are dealt with in Chapter Five, until just prior to system implementation. Discussions of such issues should feature in the systems-analysis phase, and measures to achieve security, for example, will need to be considered at the design phase. Equally, the division of analysis from design, and interface design from database design, is artificial. In any given project, it will be necessary to define boundaries to phases in order to aid in communication and the monitoring of progress, but those boundaries will need not necessarily be those adopted in this book.

Chapter One

Systems, computers, organizations and people

Systems

Before starting to consider the techniques of systems analysis and design, it is appropriate to examine the essential nature of a system, and to define the kinds of systems that the techniques outlined later in this text are intended to analyse, design and implement.

Some definitions of 'system'

(a) An assembly of components united by some form of regulated interaction to form an organized whole
(b) Any purposeful organization of resources or elements
(c) A set of instructions and rules for conducting an activity to some predetermined aim
(d) A collection of operations and procedures, men and machines by which any business activity is carried out
(e) An organized set of procedures required to accomplish a specific function.

These definitions all offer alternative perspectives on the concept of a system. In general terms, systems can be viewed as being concerned with taking inputs or resources, executing some form of regulated change and achieving results or outputs.

What is a system?

Society and nature abound in systems. Your body boasts a nervous system and a digestive system. Society organizes legal systems, political systems, educational systems, tax systems, etc. Organizations may have information-order systems, management-information systems, product-information systems and personnel-data systems. Libraries have library-housekeeping systems, information-retrieval systems and desktop-publishing systems; even the library itself may be referred to as a library system. All of these systems match one or more of the definitions given above.

Systems are identified by *elements* or *objects* within those systems, and the elements that fall within a system serve to delineate the system *boundary*. These objects have *attributes* or features.

However, on further examination of some of these systems, it becomes apparent that they are related to one another. A library-housekeeping system is, for instance, part of a library system. An invoicing system may be part of an accounting system. All systems are part of wider systems.

A system that is part of another system can be referred to as a *sub-system*. This may sound rather esoteric, but it does have practical relevance. It is important in the analysis and design of a system to recognize that system boundaries are somewhat arbitrary or subjective. It is a matter of judgement as to what functions the system should include, and which should be omitted, and it helps in overall analysis and design to be able to assign specific functions to specific systems or sub-systems.

Figure 1.1 shows a serials-control system and its sub-systems, ordering and acquisitions, cataloguing, circulation control and binding. It serves as a basis for discussion of some of the other components of systems.

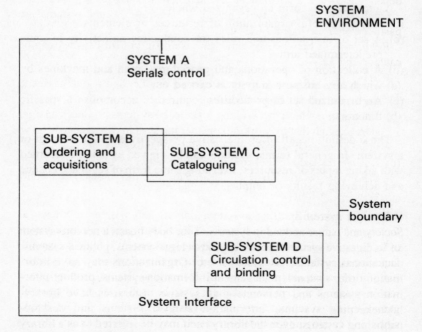

Fig. 1.1   A serials-control system

Systems are identified by their *elements*. For example, some elements in the circulation-control-and-binding sub-system might be recording issues, recalls and reservations, and renewals. The elements in a system delineate the *boundary* of that system. The choice of boundary is the systems analyst's job, and may be influenced by the time and resources available, processing methods, the structure of the organization, and a variety of other factors. Elements can belong to more than one system. You, for example, may be part of a tax system, an educational system and a political system.

Elements are linked by *relationships* or the way that one element functions in relation to another element. Relationships between systems are known as *interfaces*.

Where systems hold elements in common, there is overlap between systems. Any such overlap should be deliberate and controlled, otherwise it is likely to lead to duplication of effort. Beyond the system is its *environment*, which may be another system in its own right.

The system environment defines its *external relationships*. *Closed* systems do not interact with the environment. *Open* systems interact with the environment by taking information in and putting it out. They are dependent on the environment and sensitive to changes within it.

Open and closed are two ends of a spectrum. Many systems are partially open or partially closed.

Relationships between systems can take different forms; they can be categorized as:

(a) *Symbiotic*, where two systems operate as one, and if one ceases to exist, the other cannot function.
(b) *Synergistic*, where the working together of systems produces a larger system, such that by working together the systems are able to achieve more than each would achieve independently.
(c) *Redundant*, where there is duplication between sub-systems, such that if one specific sub-system ceased to exist, the whole system could continue without it.

The process of splitting a system into its sub-systems is known as *factoring*. This may be conducted during systems analysis, as a means of focusing on specific sub-systems. If the final system is to be successful, factoring needs to be followed by *integrating* the component sub-systems. Integration is important in drawing attention to the functioning of the whole system. The term *integration* tends to be used to allude to the amalgamation of two separate systems into one system. For example, acquisition and cataloguing may be integrated, payroll and personnel records may be integrated, despite having previously existed as separate systems.

Systems, in general, have objectives and resources and may be categorized according to both their objectives and resources.

System objectives

The general objective of any man-made system is to achieve the objectives for which the system was created. The determination of system objectives is an important component of analysis. There are four main types of system objectives which can be used to group systems into four main categories:

1 *Determined or mechanistic systems.* These systems always respond in the same way, producing the same results from any given input. Machines, in general (when reliable), are determined systems. For example, we expect a computer to respond predictably.

2 *Probalistic or stochastic systems.* A probalistic system is one where the output of any given run varies. It is not possible to predict the output of a specific run, only to specify the range of outputs that are possible and the respective probabilities of them happening. An example of a probalistic system is a library and its stock. Given a statement of the contents at one time, and of average demand, it is not possible to predict the number of items on loan at a subsequent point in time.

3 *Adaptive or self-controlled systems.* An adaptive system is one which changes and controls itself. A chemical plan with flow meters which adjust the flow of various chemicals is self-controlled. Meters measure the flow, and the flow is then adjusted or controlled to keep it within acceptable limits by the closing of valves, etc. In other words the output from the control system is fed back into the system, and influences later inputs. Adaptive systems have this type of internal *feedback* where measurements of output are used to influence subsequent inputs.

4 *Competitive or externally controlled systems.* Much of the business world is comprised of competitive or externally controlled systems. These systems are controlled by external factors in the systems environment. Such factors cause the system to change. For example, in a production system, if a product does not sell, then the product and the production system must be modified: this is a reaction to market pressures. If a library service, such as a mobile library, is underutilized, then modifications will be made to that service.

System resources

There are two types of system resources:

● Those that will be changed into output
● Those that are used to effect the change.

Real physical production and distribution systems are concerned primarily with the first kind of resources. They need however to be accompanied by information systems which keep records of the production and distribution activities. Information systems use resources in the second category and are used to effect the change. Many computer systems are concerned with record-keeping for other systems, such as production systems, issue systems and medical systems. Our focus here is on information systems, but it would be dangerous to neglect the systems to which the information systems pertain, since it is important to understand the purpose of the information in the information system.

Change activity

Systems may also be characterized by the way in which they process inputs to produce outputs. This process can be described as the change activity. The method of change activity has a significant impact on the efficiency of processing. Any system is likely to have rules which govern the change activity.

Change activities comprise processes and decisions. The rules which govern the change activity must determine:

● Which processes and decisions are encompassed by the system
● The sequences in which these processes and decisions are to be performed
● The direct limits and constraints on the system
● The resources necessary to achieve the change activity
● The change-activity environment, including its physical environment and its systems environment (covering, for instance, related systems).

Conclusion

These few ideas and definitions which consider systems in general terms are intended to encourage the reader to examine the systems around him and to provide a language for describing systems.

This first section has avoided the temptation to focus more narrowly on computer systems, and has emphasized that systems abound, but only a small proportion of these lend themselves to computerization.

The systems which represent the subject of this book are the computerized information systems with which the information professional is likely to have contact. These include information-retrieval systems, library-housekeeping systems, word-processing and text-management systems, and management-information systems.

Within the framework identified in this section a number of key problem areas emerge:

- Identification of the whole system and its boundaries
- Dealing with problems associated with the system interfaces
- Maintaining the system's dynamic interaction with its environment
- Resolving conflicting systems objectives.

The information system associated with an organization must help to achieve integration of its sub-systems. These systems must meet organizational objectives, promote integration of activities and facilitate control.

System life-cycles

A system life-cycle can be viewed as comprising six stages, as in Figure 1.2. After a system has been designed and introduced, it will evolve during an operating phase. Eventually, the system will become less effective than it was initially, either because of mechanical or other faults, or because the system environment has changed and the system is not able to evolve to meet the changes in the environment. Decay may also be speeded in an environment where a new system is being planned. The last stage in the system life-cycle is its replacement. The duration of each stage will vary from one system to another. The duration of the analysis, design, and implementation phases will vary between systems.

Indeed the duration of individual steps within the analysis-and-design process will vary from a few hours or days to two or three years. Nevertheless, in general, the operating-evolution phase should be the longest, possibly lasting a number of years. The life of computer systems is relatively short. Changes in both the environment and the technology contribute to the decay and eventual replacement of computer systems.

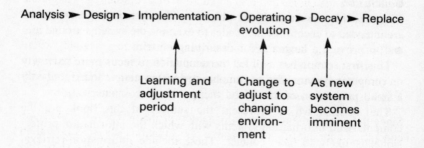

Fig. 1.2 A system life-cycle

When to use systems analysis and design

Systems analysis and design is, as we have already noted, an approach which aids in the effective implementation of computer systems.

To be more specific, then, systems analysis and design may be employed whenever a new computer-based system is being contemplated. This includes:

- Replacement of manual systems with computerized systems
- Changeover from one computerized system to another (e.g. from batch to online operation, or from a system based on a shared mainframe to a system based on a locally controlled microcomputer or minicomputer)
- Modifications, upgrades and extensions to the existing computer-based system (offering, for example, new functions such as online public-access catalogues).

In the early days of computer-based systems, most systems-analysis-and-design exercises were concerned with the first of the above alternatives. Now, most exercises deal with either the second or third situation above, and changeovers and upgrades have become a regular feature of the operation of computer-based systems. All too often, an organization may be involved in an upgrade in one system supporting part of its operations and, possibly, renewing another system for another part of its operation simultaneously.

Several systems-analysis-and-design exercises may be running simultaneously, although out of phase with each other, and on different scales. Systems analysis and design may be employed in two distinct circumstances:

- To aid in the choice and implementation of a commercially available pre-packaged system. The system may include hardware or software or both.
- To aid in the design and implementation of a new system, where a system's designer will be responsible for selecting the hardware on which a system is to run and specifying and writing programs to create the system.

Since the librarian and other information professionals will chiefly be concerned with the first of the above two situations, the selection of an existing package, the account which follows emphasizes the steps that are necessary in this process. Some information professionals may, however, be involved in some aspects of the design of a system, and thus, design is also considered.

The systems-analysis-and-design project

Systems analysis and design offers a strategy for the introduction of computer-based systems. There are a number of possible models for a systems-analysis-and-design exercise, but the standard exercise involves five stages which are outlined below.

It is suggested that most organizations will progress through these various stages, although in some systems exercises, some stages may be subdivided or amalgamated, depending on the scale of the exercise. Nevertheless, with the outline given below it is possible to model and agree a strategy for system choice and implementation.

As outlined here, the five phases assume that the selection process proceeds from software to hardware, rather than vice versa. At one time the availability of software and hardware was such that the hardware restricted the choice of software. Now, for most applications, it would normally be sensible to define requirements, choose software and proceed to choose hardware.

The five stages are:

- Definition of objectives
- Definition of systems requirements
- Design phase
- Implementation phase
- Evaluation phase.

The first two of these phases can be grouped together as systems analysis (see also Figure 1.3).

Definition of objectives	Terms of reference developed; initial needs analysis as a study proposal; leads to feasibility study, including evaluation of options, and analysis of existing systems.
Definition of systems requirements	Specification of systems requirements.
Design phase	Logical systems model; physical systems model; choice and ordering of hardware and software configuration.
Implementation phase	Planning and preparation; education and training; database creation; system installation; switchover.
Evaluation phase	Initial evaluation; ongoing monitoring; maintenance; evolution.

Fig. 1.3 Summary of stages in systems analysis and design

Definition of objectives

A suggestion that a new system might solve problems and offer oppportunities for new developments is not a sufficient basis for launching into a computerized project. The first step must be to hold discussions to refine the objectives of any new system.

This phase is valuable both in evolving guidelines and requirements which will be invaluable later in the project, and in commencing the communication process and ensuring that all points of view are considered from the very beginning, and that early agreement and support for changes are achieved. It is clearly important at this stage to establish the various project committees, to start discussions with trade unions, and to involve all interested parties. This phase should review established practices and procedures and attempt to identify where, when, why and how a computer-based system might be helpful. An initial needs analysis should be conducted, in cooperation with those staff whose activities are likely to be affected by the system, and should culminate in a written specification of the terms of reference for more detailed work, in the form of a study proposal.

If the study proposal is accepted by management, more detailed investigation of the existing system or problem area will take the form of a feasibility study. The purpose of the feasibility study is to establish the system options that are available, and to define the resources needed to complete the detailed investigations which might follow.

The next step is to start to gather information on how to achieve the objectives identified during the first phase. This stage is essentially about information gathering, both from internal and external sources. The information collected should facilitate a decision about the type of system that is available to meet the requirements of the organization. Possible conclusions are that: a local software package needs to be developed; cooperative system development with another information-management organization or library or group thereof is the most attractive option; or a turnkey package should be selected.

This stage is unlikely to lead directly to the selection of a specific system although if there are very special requirements or severe hardware constraints, there may only be one system which is satisfactory. Normally, general directions and a group of possible systems will be identified for further consideration. It is important to collect as much information as possible from as many sources as possible, and to build up well-organized files of information for all committee members and other interested parties to consult.

Clearly, software houses and other suppliers of systems are important at this stage. Also directories that review systems and various other special sources, such as the Library Technology Centre, may provide valuable assistance. Workshops offered by professional associations, educational institutions, exhibitions and conferences are all valuable. If at all possible, other librarians and information managers with experience with computerized systems should be visited, telephoned and generally consulted whenever the opportunity arises.

A reputable system vendor will be prepared to put potential customers in contact with other users. At some stage during the collection of information, when it becomes reasonably clear what is likely to be available, it would be wise to evolve, from the objectives identified in the first phase, a preliminary check-list of features of systems that might be of particular interest. Various directories of software packages, turnkey systems and hardware include check-lists, which can be used as a model for the evolution of a local check-list. The check-list will facilitate purposive sifting of the information gathered, and will make decisions easier to arrive at. Both hardware and software aspects should be considered.

In addition to gathering information concerning systems options, this phase may involve the development of a logical system description for the existing system. If the existing system is already well understood and well documented, or, alternatively will be superseded by a new system which offers completely different functions from the old system, then it may be unnecessary to investigate the existing system further. If, however, the new system must perform many of the same processes as the old system, then an analysis of the existing system is a useful prerequisite to the in-depth study of user requirements which leads to the logical design of the new system.

If a new system is to be designed, a feasibility study may involve assessing specific aspects of any potential system, and possibly building small trial sub-systems.

Definition of systems requirements (investigation and specification of requirements)

With more complete knowledge of the options available and some insight into how the various solutions might be applied to meet the requirements in a specific application, it is necessary to go back and develop a full system specification. Typically, a definition phase should seek to answer questions such as:

- Which operations is the system to cover?
- Which databases need to be created?
- How are these databases to be created?

- What kind of records are to be in the databases?
- What information will be sought from the database?
- How will the information sought from the file be presented?
- Which are the vital features and which are merely desirable additions?
- Who will use the system regularly?
- What level of experience can be expected of users?

The definition phase will lead naturally into the design phase.

Design phase (detailed design and programming)

If new software is to be written, the design phase is concerned with the analysis, flowcharting, and other charting of the functions and operations that the system must perform, prior to the programs being written.

When an existing turnkey system or software package is to be selected, such a detailed analysis is not normally necessary, although a detailed system specification is essential as a basis for the final selection of the package, and to provide the groundwork for the implementation of the system. The detailed specification should outline all of the features required in the system, and is important in negotiations with the system supplier.

If a large turnkey system for, say, library housekeeping is under consideration, an invitation to tender will be issued at this stage to a limited number (say three to six) of systems suppliers. These suppliers will be required to submit a quotation against the specification by a particular date. Where separate pieces of hardware and software are being acquired from different suppliers, a number of quotations may need to be gathered. In this situation the systems librarian needs to be very clear as to the specification of the hardware and software for which he is being quoted. This phase can be particularly difficult when implementing, say, a medium-sized microcomputer installation, where the system is not pre-packaged and the number of options for hardware and software combinations may be matched only by the variety of different discount arrangements available from different suppliers. Some libraries are in organizations, such as local authorities, where there is a specific tendering procedure which must be followed, and where legal assistance may be available in drafting contracts.

When bids have been received, or with smaller systems, as quotations are being negotiated, systems should be demonstrated by their suppliers. Demonstrations for large systems should preferably be on-site (e.g. in the library), and should certainly permit a number of the staff who will be affected by the new system to inspect the proposed one. Demonstrations facilitate communication, and can be used as an opportunity for staff who will be included in the day-to-day running of the system to learn a little about it and to ask questions. After the demonstrations, further discussions should lead to the choice of system, including hardware and software and, subsequently, orders must be placed, contracts signed, etc.

Implementation phase

Normally, once orders have been placed there will be a lull whilst the information manager waits to see whether delivery dates will be met. This time should be spent in planning the installation and implementation of the system. The installation phase starts with a review of the way in which the system will affect the existing operations of the organization. If a thorough analysis has been performed in the earlier stages of the systems-analysis exercise, many of the jobs, issues and other matters concerned with the installation of the system will have been identified and planned already. At this point it is necessary to gather a quantitative picture of the work to be done in order to achieve implementation, and to identify specific staff responsibilities.

A detailed timetable of training, installation, and other activities needs to be agreed and finalized. The timetable should cover the various aspects of implementation, as discussed below. The order of treatment is not significant. Indeed, many of these activities may be proceeding in parallel.

1 *Preparation and planning.* Various preparatory activities may be necessary. Although most of these issues should already have been thoroughly discussed, any new factors or options that were left open should be examined. The forms of records and files for various applications and databases need to be finalized. The sites for any central computer installation and for any workstations will need to be prepared and appropriate telecommunication links installed.

2 *Install hardware.* Including both the computer itself and the various workstations, as well as other peripherals and links to telecommunication networks.

3 *Install software.* Once the hardware has been installed, the next stage is to install the software, run it, and test it on small trial databases.

4 *Create databases.* Once it is clear that the hardware and software are performing satisfactorily, work must begin on the construction of the full databases for the system. The records for the databases may be derived from a variety of different sources.

Procedures must be established for the creation of records for new items, including for example, new borrowers, new books, new citations, new personnel. If a circulation-control system is being implemented, book labelling (with bar codes) can be a major task.

5 *Staff training* and the preparation of appropriate check-lists, instruction and reference manuals are important in successful implementation of a system.

6 *Implement system* or move into full operation of the system. This may simply be a matter of making the system, with its supporting literature, available. However, if other functions depend upon the system or if the system involves a number of modules it may be sensible to phase its introduction in various areas of application.

Evaluation phase (maintenance and review)

The last stage of a systems-analysis exercise is a long way from the initial establishment of requirements, but it is nevertheless important to emphasize that after successful implementation it is necessary to complete the exercise by going back to the specification and assessing the extent to which the system is meeting its stated objectives. Such an assessment may lead to improvements and refinements in the way in which a system is used.

Participation in user groups or cooperatives (for software packages and turnkey systems) may also assist in the process of formulating evaluative comments about the system, and pressing for changes from the system designer or supplier. Such groups can also be a means of maintaining a sound relationship with the system supplier.

People in systems analysis and design

The purpose of this section is to emphasize from the start that people have control over computer systems (for the moment at least!) and that computer systems are for people.

There are many different people involved in the design of a computerized system. The systems analyst is a key figure. Systems analysts do not however work alone.

They work alongside the people for whom they are designing or implementing a system. Such people may be professionals from a variety of different fields, and may include librarians, information managers, accountants, doctors, managers and office supervisors. Indeed, with appropriate training, members of these groups are in a strong position to, and may need to, conduct part of the systems-analysis-and-design process. They certainly need to be able to understand how a systems project might proceed through analysis, design and implementation.

Systems-analysis-and-design exercises may be conducted on smaller or larger systems, over differing timescales, and requiring different levels of commitment on the part of staff. Nevertheless, in every situation there must be staff who are responsible for both central control and decision-making, and getting the work done.

For large projects, central control will normally be vested in a committee, possibly dubbed the Project Management Committee. Senior management, together with various other interested parties, must be represented on this committee. Representatives will be selected in accordance with the project being undertaken and from different levels of the hierarchy. Trade-union representatives are also important, as is the systems analyst or systems librarian. Whilst it is unwise for the Project Management Committee to be too large, it must be recognized that a variety of representatives with different views and experience can help to ensure that planning covers all eventualities.

The role of the Project Management Committee is to:

- Direct the project
- Monitor the progress of the project
- Facilitate communication about the project's progress.

The day-to-day execution of the Project Management Committee's decisions is the task of the systems analyst or, in libraries, the systems librarian, and, when appropriate, their teams. These specialists work together with other staff whose work will be affected by the new system. The systems analyst is important as a source of expertise in computer systems and their applications, and offers information and advice to the Project Management Committee. Also, the systems analyst has more time available to direct the implementation of new systems than would a member of staff with other significant management responsibilities.

The systems analyst

In a large organization, at least one full-time member of staff needs to be appointed to have responsibility for computer systems. Sometimes, as in a large company or local authority, a complete department may be devoted to systems analysis and design. At the other extreme, a small organization may not be able to keep a full-time, permanent systems analyst occupied. Here, a consultant may be asked to assist with a specific project.

The task of a systems analyst is to:

- Investigate and assimilate information about the way in which a system currently operates
- Analyse its performance in the light of the system objectives which are identified by management
- Develop and evaluate ideas about how the system can be improved or reorganized

- Design in detail a new system meeting the requirements that have been identified
- Implement the new system once it has been developed.

The central role of the systems analyst is as an intermediary between the user and the computer system, viz.

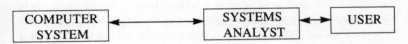

In accomplishing these tasks the systems analyst is required to act as an intermediary between the computer system and programmers and other computer professionals and the system user.

This role as intermediary has different facets, some of which reinforce one another but others of which may be difficult to achieve simultaneously. The systems analyst is required to act as:

(a) *Catalyst* for change, by providing users with the opportunity to examine their job, problems and potential solutions

(b) *Adviser*, who offers advice about what can be achieved with the computer system (and not what can't be achieved!).

(c) *Educator*, to educate and widen people's knowledge and horizons concerning computer systems and systems methodologies, with particular attention to those who have difficulty in understanding or relating to technology.

(d) *Salesman*, to sell ideas to users and managers. Achievements depend to some extent on the users' being committed to the system and making it work. Positive attitudes need to be cultivated.

(e) *Communicator*, a central function. Communication involves both input and output. Listening and reading are at least as important as talking and writing. The systems analyst must communicate effectively with users at all levels, management, external bodies such as hardware suppliers, technical staff, programmers, computer-operations staff, and other systems analysts.

(f) *Agent of change*. The systems analyst will be seen as an agent of change. This can provoke resistance, as discussed in the next section.

With this range of different activities and roles the systems analyst must possess appropriate personal qualities, skills and knowledge.

The systems analyst must be able to communicate well, and evaluate ideas objectively and formulate ideas independently. They must be acceptable to all levels, good listeners, confident and unbiased. In designing systems, analysts must be patient and perceptive, careful and yet creative. They must be objective and unbiased, with logical minds and a methodical approach.

Alongside these personal qualities the analyst must have certain skills. They must be able to recognize, describe, define and analyse a problem. They must have the ability to present ideas clearly, in both written and spoken form. They must be equally at home with numbers and words and, above all, they must be able to complete tasks under pressures of time, money, politics, personalities and technological change.

Clearly personality and skills, whilst essential are not sufficient. It is necessary that the analyst have the appropriate knowledge. The analyst needs to know about:

● Computer systems
● Systems analysis and design
● The application area to which the system is being applied.

Some awareness of various other additional areas such as operations research, organization theory and practice, industrial sociology and physiology, ergonomics, accountancy and economics would also be useful.

System users

Systems analysis, design and implementation are concerned with the analysis, design and implementation of systems for people. Good communication is essential for effective fact-finding, and later for successful design and implementation. People may be apprehensive about change, and may need to be persuaded that the new system is worthwhile and will improve the way in which they can achieve certain activities. Any resistance to change must be overcome. A first step in handling resistance is to understand the forces that motivate people to any activity, work and pursuit. The chief motivating forces for most people fall into one or more of the following categories:

(a) The need to satisfy physiological needs, for food, shelter, rest, variety, safety and sex, is most basic, although may be well removed from people's reasons for interacting with computer systems. Nevertheless most people view their work as a means of fulfilling these basic needs.

(b) The need to feel safe and secure against any danger and against any loss of physiological satisfaction.

(c) Social needs, such as the needs of association, acceptance by associates and giving and receiving friendship.

(d) Ego needs, including recognition, sense of achievement, prestige, job satisfaction, opportunities to realize one's potential and to be creative.

If people feel that their ability to satisfy one of these needs is threatened by change, they may seek to resist that change. They may also feel that any proposed change constitutes implied criticism of the way in which they have always tackled a job, and may be suspicious of the motives for change.

Insecurity engendered by the unknown or possible job loss or the need to learn new skills may also worry an employee in a changing working environment. If people do not wish to go along with change they may disagree with new proposals, by adopting one of the following stances:

Ground rules for resisting persuasion
1 Don't listen.
2 Convince yourself and others that the persuader has ulterior motives, preferably behind the persuader's back.
3 Generate a real dislike for the analyst.
4 Exaggerate any objections.
5 Raise the temperature of the discussion, so that both sides lose their tempers.
6 Discuss and preferably criticize personalities, not issues.
7 Don't tell anyone your real objections.
8 Hang on to your prejudices.

When faced with this barrage of tactics, the systems analyst needs an approach which overcomes resistance to change. Central planks of this strategy are:

Ground rules for combating resistance
1 Keep people informed, giving them reasons for the change, and emphasizing the positive and beneficial aspects of change.
2 Let people participate in planning and implementation, and ensure that they can see that their suggestions have been acted upon, where appropriate.
3 Give people time to accept new ideas. Be prepared to discuss and persuade and negotiate. A mutually satisfactory solution must be achieved. If necessary, present and discuss alternative strategies.
4 Avoid arguments, by sticking to essentials and resisting the temptation to discuss personalities, or to re-live the past.
5 Listen sympathetically to any problems, and be ready to admit and acknowledge any difficulties, whilst at the same time stressing advantages and benefits. Ask for suggestions for overcoming problems.

6   Cultivate the habit of change. People can be acclimatized to change, by working in an environment where change is common.
7   Give security by offering appropriate training and support and making sure that people know that it is available.
8   Give financial and employment security as far as possible.
9   Make jobs varied, and where monotonous tasks must be completed, intersperse them with other more interesting activities. Make jobs as challenging as the people involved will appreciate.
10 Emphasize attempts to save unnecessary effort, improve the service, etc.
11 Keep your sense of humour and objectivity.

Information-systems methodologies

What is an information-systems methodology?

An information-systems methodology is a methodical approach to information-systems planning, analysis and design. A *methodology* is a body of methods, rules and postulates employed by a discipline.

Information-systems methodologies have been developed by systems analysts and designers as a tool to aid in modelling information systems and designing a computer-based system which meets the requirements of the users of the information. They assist in efficient and effective systems analysis and contribute to effective systems and software design and development. Information-systems methodologies have not been designed to assist the user of a computer system to specify requirements, although there are good reasons why such a user might borrow some of the tools and approaches of the recognized methodologies to assist in a systematic analysis of requirements and specification of a system.

Certainly, where a large and complex system is being considered, the adoption of a clearly defined methodology may well lead to more effective systems.

In relation to software development, Aktas (1987) tabulates some properties of a structured information system (Figure 1.4). These would appear to be desirable characteristics of any system implementation, whether the system is being written specifically for a given application or whether a standard package is being adopted and tailored. Analysis and design problems in implementing a standard package for a given library may not be so complex as those associated with the development of a new system, but they still exist.

acceptable	logical/hierarchical
better documented	low coupling
better tested	maintainable
cohesive	modular
comparable	more reliable
economical	observable/visible
efficient	simple
fast development rate	timely
feasible	uniform
flexible	user friendly

Fig. 1.4 Some properties of a structured information system

A methodology is valuable not only in organizing and structuring information, but also in achieving a complete and correct set of information requirements from the people who will make use of the system. It may be difficult to elicit such a statement of requirements. Davis gives three reasons for such a difficulty:

● The limitation of human beings as information processors and problem solvers
● The variety and complexity of information requirements
● The complex patterns of interaction among users and analysts in defining requirements.

Add to these inherent limitations the other problems identified in Chapter One, and it is not difficult to see that the acquisition of a sound set of systems requirements in which to base systems design is not an easy task.

There are a number of different methodologies available on the market, each offering different features, and encompassing different aspects of the systems-analysis, design and implementation process. Figure 1.5 summarizes the components that should be present in a methodology.

Structured information systems methodologies
The more established systems methodologies can all be regarded as *structured methodologies*.

All structured methodologies hold some features in common. They all use graphical models, place emphasis on user communication and involve repetition of the previous phase(s), step(s) and reviews. In structural analysis and design the models represent the functions of the system rather than how to accomplish them. Emphasis is on the logical components of the system rather than its physical components.

Information-system methodologies can be divided into three main groups:

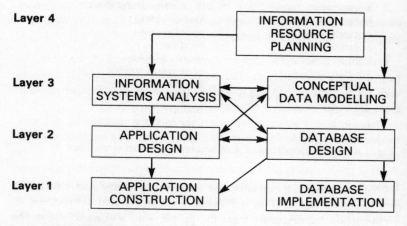

Fig. 1.5 **Methodology components**

1 *Functional decomposition methodologies*, e.g. top-down approach; bottom-up approach; HIPO (hierarchy plus input-process-output); stepwise refinement approach; information-hiding approach.

Functional decomposition methodologies emphasize the dissection of a system into smaller sub-systems, so that these are not so complex to understand, design and implement.

2 *Data- and process-oriented methodologies* can be split broadly into two groups although some methodologies have elements of both:

(a) *Data-oriented methodologies*, e.g. structured analysis and design technique (SADT); composite design; structured design; structured systems analysis (SSA); structured systems analysis and design methodology (SSADM); LBMS systems and development method (LSDM).

(b) *Process-oriented methodologies*, e.g. Jackson system development (JSD); structured analysis design and implementation of computer systems (STRADIS); Warnier/Orr methodology; information engineering (IEM); Jordan structured analysis and system specification (SASS).

Data-oriented methodologies mainly emphasize the characteristics of the data to be processed. Dataflow-oriented methodologies are based on decomposition of a system into modules by considering the types of data elements and their logical behaviour within the system. Data-structure-oriented methodologies mainly emphasize the input/output data structures of the system.

3   *Prescriptive methodologies*, e.g. Chapin's approach; design by objectives (DBO); problem analysis diagram (PAD); problem statement language (PSL)/problem statement analysis (PSA).

Prescriptive methodologies are generally computerized procedures to help software development. The major objective is to provide analysts with a prescriptive approach to analyse the system specification and free them from the detailed technicalities of program design.

This list amply demonstrates that there are a number of different methodologies. It is, however, useful to adopt one methodology as standard within an organization.

All of these methodologies are distinct, but they do have some common features. They all use structured tools. A shared property of these tools is that many are graphical. Another characteristic of most of the structured tools is that they are based on the tree concept. Many of the tools are characteristic components of their respective systems-development methodologies. Some such tools are hierarchy charts, dataflow diagrams, structure charts and Warnier/Orr diagrams.

Which methodology?

If indeed it is possible to evaluate or compare the above methodologies or any other methodology used in systems analysis, then it is necessary to be able to measure the quality of the analysis or the resultant specification. No established criteria exist for analysing the quality of a system, although there is much current research in this area. Aktas (1982) proposed three groups of metrics relating to the structure, completeness and resource characteristics of information systems. More specifically these are:

(a)   *Structural characteristics*: reliability; performance; applicability; relative complexity; compiling; cohesion; design logic and presentation clarity; security and protection
(b)   *Completeness characteristics*: relative requirements; documentation; completeness
(c)   *Resource characteristics*: necessary equipment; cost effectiveness.

Some of these are more important than others in a given systems implementation, and equally some are easier to measure than others. Nevertheless, this list does perhaps offer some practical pointers for systems evaluation, which might be applied both in evaluating the systems methodology and in evaluating the final system itself.

Methodology adopted here

Whilst information-systems methodologies are important and the tools that they offer should be exploited where possible, there are a number of different methodologies and it is difficult to choose between these. This text does not adopt any of the proprietary methodologies currently available in the commercial market-place. There are two main reasons for this:

- None of the methodologies has been demonstrated to be applicable in all development circumstances. Most of them tend to be more relevant to large organizations with significant computer resources and undertaking complex projects.
- This means that none of these methodologies is suitable for general education. This book rather draws together some of the techniques that are common to many methodologies, and attempts to introduce some of the basic tools for systems analysis and design.

Some, for example Heseltine, would argue that a systems-analysis exercise based on a structured methodology is not appropriate in a situation where the information professional is constrained to select a solution from one of a very limited number of available systems. Certainly the information professional must consider the methodology that needs to be adopted to support the selection, design and implementation of a system, and in many circumstances only some of the techniques and approaches outlined in the later chapters of this book will be appropriate. Different applications demand different approaches, and the techniques and methodologies to be adopted need to be established early in the consideration of plans for a new computer system.

Further reading

Aktas, Z., *Structured analysis and design of information systems*, London, Prentice-Hall, 1987.

Aktas, Z., *Discussion of structured systems analysis and design strategies for information systems*; paper presented at the ACM Tenth Annual Computer Science Conference, Indianapolis, February 1982.

Davis, G. B., 'Strategies for information requirements determination', *IBM systems journal*, 21 (1), 1982, 4−30.

Heseltine, R., 'Finding out what they're all about: the function of the library system specification', *IT news*, 19, May 1989, 50−2.

Holloway, S., *Methodology handbook for information managers*, Aldershot, Gower Technical, 1989.

National Computing Centre, *Introducing systems analysis and design*, Manchester, National Computing Centre, 1978.

Olle, T. W. and others, *Information system methodologies: a framework for understanding*, Wokingham, Addison-Wesley, 1988.

Smith, D., *Systems thinking in library and information management*, London, Bingley, 1980.

Waters, S. J., *Systems specifications*, Manchester, National Computing Centre, 1981.

Chapter Two

Systems analysis and modelling

Introduction

This chapter focuses on those techniques associated with systems *analysis*. In general the term analysis is used to describe the process of looking at something that already exists. The design of an information system is often a process of re-design. If a good system already exists, then the emphasis in design will be on everything that the existing system does and computerizing or re-computerizing it more effectively. If there is no existing system, or a poor existing system, then analysis is likely to be a more major exercise. In a typical situation, some parts of existing systems are likely to be better defined and more successful than others, so that a typical project will be a mixture of analysis and design. It is difficult to make a sharp distinction between analysis and design, since analysis forms a basis for design and the transition from analysis to design is not clear cut.

This chapter then focuses on those techniques and issues that are important in analysis, but some are also applicable to the design stages of the project, whilst some of the techniques in Chapters Three and Four may also be appropriate in analysis. The techniques covered in this chapter may be applied both in the analysis of existing systems, and also in the analysis of requirements leading to a logical design for a new system.

The system specification

The objective of the analysis phase of a systems-analysis-and-design exercise is the establishment of the requirements for the system that is to be acquired, developed and installed.

The analysis and logical design of a system can be summarized in a system specification or specification of operational requirements (O/R). This document records the features that are required of the system. The Central Computer and Telecommunications Agency (CCTA) has described an O/R as:

The statement issued to suppliers giving details of a project against which they are invited to submit proposals. It is an important document which must enable the supplier to determine whether or not he should invest effort in competing for the business.

Some organizations lay down specific procedures for any computer-procurement exercise. The CCTA procedures are widely used for large purchases. It is essential to check whether any procurement procedures are laid down by the organization and to adhere to these.

The precise nature of the system specification must depend upon its function. A specification produced for the design of a system within an organization may focus primarily on the functional specification of a system. A requirements specification that is submitted to turnkey-systems suppliers and other external suppliers must be wider ranging, and should summarize the environment and context within which hardware and software are required to work in order to function as a system. Typically, such a specification might include:

(a) Appropriate background information about the organization
(b) Details of the facilities to be provided by a computerized system, including which of these are mandatory and which are desirable
(c) Details of the environment within which the system will operate, including standards (e.g. MARC), communication protocols and health and safety regulations
(d) The size of the system, in terms of: numbers of records to be handled, numbers of work stations required, likely transaction rate, growth rates
(e) A timetable for the implementation of the system
(f) Mandatory questions to be answered by suppliers, in order that basic information on their systems may be established, e.g. size of hardware, electrical requirements, system support arrangements, costs
(g) Information concerning any special constraints such as timetabling problems, or the need to link system introduction to the building of a new library
(h) Information about terms or form of contract and any acceptance tests.

There are four golden rules to recognize in drafting a system specification:

1 Don't dictate to suppliers how to meet the requirements. The design is the responsibility of the supplier.
2 Don't base requirements on the knowledge of one particular system.
3 Be realistic in stating requirements. Ideally, a system specification

should reflect the kind of systems that will be available on the market six months after it is written. In other words, the specification should ask for state-of-the-art technology and a *little* more, if this is appropriate for the application.

4 Take costs into account in specifying requirements.

Budgetary constraints may be recorded in a systems specification, or the organization may prefer not to disclose these.

The system-requirements specification has three fundamental roles:

(a) *As a communication document* to aid in: communication with staff; communication with systems suppliers; communication, discussion, development and crystallization amongst the project team; management approval and decision-making
(b) *As a reference document* for the project team during implementation and later maintenance and review
(c) *As a legal document* as part of the contract with the supplier
(d) *To aid in the systematic and objective comparison* of alternative systems that might possibly meet the systems requirements.

Different levels of detail may be appropriate for specifications for different applications. Nevertheless, the specification is an important document in that it has a role to play throughout the life-cycle of the system as summarized in Figure 2.1.

Analysis	Development of the system-requirements specification (SRS) aids in clarification and communication concerning requirements.
Design	Use of SRS in design and selection of system and in negotiation with suppliers.
Implementation	Use of SRS as a guide to implementation.
Operating evolution	A reference document against which evaluation can be performed.
Decay	SRS helps to identify causes of decay.
Replacement	SRS may form the basis for a new analysis project and for consideration of requirements and necessity for a new system.

Fig. 2.1 Use of requirements specification in system life-cycle

System specification objectives

Objectives that need to be considered in relation to any computer system and are likely to feature in the specification include:

- *Efficiency* in use of computing resources
- *Timeliness* so that turnaround and response times are met
- *Reliability* so that breakdowns are minimized and the system recovers from breakdowns quickly and without long-lasting effects
- *Accuracy* so that the system works at an acceptable level of correctness
- *Compatibility* so that the system interfaces with existing and future computer systems
- *Implementability* so that the system can be implemented fully within the available resources
- *Maintainability* so that the system will be modifiable with respect to continuing resources
- *Flexibility* so that the system can cater for change
- *Portability* so that the system can cope with changes in hardware/software configurations
- *Economy* so that the system is cost-effective or cost-beneficial when compared with its alternatives.

Fact-finding techniques

Fact finding or gathering is central to any analysis of requirements. Indeed much of analysis is concerned with what facts to find, how to find those facts, and, then, how to record them. Before embarking on any fact-finding exercise it is important to recognize that:

(a) Facts do not emerge in neat bundles. The relevant facts may need to be gathered from a variety of sources, and sifted from less relevant facts.

(b) It is impossible ever to be confident that fact finding is complete. Although analysis is the main phase during which fact gathering is conducted, fact gathering will also be necessary during design and implementation phases.

Fact-recording techniques prompt what facts to find and give the protocols for modelling them. Thus standards which offer guidance as to the data to be recorded direct fact finding by requiring that standard documents and diagrams must be completed. Standards are useful in aiding analysis and design, documenting the results of analysis and communicating those results to other people.

Background reading

Background reading is often the first phase of any analysis exercise. The analyst may already have a good grasp of the existing organization and its practices and procedures. If however this is not the case, it is necessary that the analyst familiarize himself with the objectives, activities and functions of the organization in which the computer system is to be implemented. Typical sources of information that can usefully be perused include:

● Organization charts
● Administrative-procedure manuals
● Job descriptions and specifications
● Training manuals and memoranda
● Sales and promotional literature.

It is important not to waste too much time on background reading, as this activity can easily become poorly directed and time-consuming, but some consideration of existing documents must be undertaken before moving on to other fact-gathering techniques.

Existing records may help to establish quantitative information about volumes, frequencies, trends and ratios that is not readily available during interviews, and may bring to light issues or factors that are overlooked during interviews.

Interviewing

The objective of early interviews is two-fold:

● To discover facts about procedures and decisions
● To meet staff and establish early communication.

Effective interviewing is a skill that develops with practice. It is important that interviews are conducted effectively. First interviews, in particular, leave strong impressions. Later interviews may be concerned with:

● Checking the analyst's understanding of system operations
● Validating aspects of a proposed system design
● Building confidence in the new system.

Interviewing involves two main activities on the part of the interviewer: listening and explaining.

Interviewers are an effective method of fact gathering since a high response rate can be expected. The two-way communication that is established during the interview is less likely to lead to misunderstanding and more likely to offer a complete picture of the situation, than other methods.

Preparation

Prior to conducting any interview, time must be devoted to planning. During planning the following must be established:

(a) The objective of the interview. This should be clearly specified, and made known to all concerned. The objective can be expanded into a series of points on which information should be exchanged.

(b) Background information, such as names, jobs, purpose of jobs, why this person is being interviewed.

(c) The time, duration and venue of the interview must be arranged, and be mutually convenient. On some occasions it will be appropriate to conduct the interview in the work place; on others the interview may be less hindered by interruption etc. if it is conducted away from the work place.

(d) Authorization for the interview. It is important that the manager's permission is granted before his staff are interviewed. Indeed, an appropriate place to start interviewing is often the top of the hierarchy. Managers are likely to proffer useful information on the objectives of the system and perceptions concerning the new system, even if they have little information to offer on its day-to-day running.

Conducting the interview − a checklist

1 Be punctual, observe elementary good manners and dress appropriately.

2 Make sure that both parties are seated.

3 Offer a clear introduction and explanation of the purpose of the interview at the start.

4 Control the interview, and steer a happy medium between achieving the planned objectives of the interview and allowing the interviewee to offer additional, unexpected information.

5 Ask questions to which the interviewee can be expected to know the answers.

6 Use the interviewee's terminology as far as possible, and avoid introducing your own jargon.

7 Make the interview impersonal and objective. Any comments on existing practices should be complimentary and encouraging rather than critical. The interviewer should show interest and warmth.

8 Listen most of the time, and watch gestures, facial expressions, eye contact and general posture of the interviewee.

9 Do not waste time; ensure that the duration of the interview is as planned. If necessary arrange a second interview.

10   Conclude with a brief friendly exchange to smooth later relation-
     ships.
11   Write notes up immediately afterwards, and submit these to the inter-
     viewee for approval.
12   Group interviews together so that the analyst can focus attention
     on this data-gathering activity and can adopt a consistent approach
     to each interviewee.

On occasions it may be necessary to use more than one interviewer in
order to complete all interviews in a reasonable period of time. In these
circumstances coordination is essential. Interviewers must be adequately
briefed and need to keep to an agreed set of questions. The format of
the record of the interview must also be carefully controlled, so that data
can be integrated from a number of different interviews.

Recording interviews

Recording an interview is a daunting task. Much of the information that
is conveyed can be converted into models of the organization or the
system. The remaining information, on matters such as opinion, worries
and requirements, will need to be minuted to form a record for future
reference. A discussion-record document can be used to summarize the
meetings that take place as the project progresses.

Questionnaires

Questionnaires can be used to gather certain kinds of data during a
systems-analysis study. They are not as popular as interviews because:

- They are prone to low response rates
- Questions may be answered and interpreted by the respondents in
  different ways
- There is no opportunity to clarify ambiguities in the way in which the
  questionnaire has been completed, unless a follow-up visit or
  telephone call is made
- The analyst will not be able to collect peripheral information by
  observing the user's work place or work practices
- It is more difficult to discern or influence attitudes by questionnaire.
  Unlike an interview, a questionnaire does little to establish a
  communication process between analyst and user, and to encourage
  active participation on the part of the user.

On the other hand, there are circumstances in which questionnaires can
be useful. If users are scattered and it is impossible to visit all sites, either
because of time or distance, then a questionnaire may elicit a quick

response from a large number of people. Questionnaires may also be used to identify 'key' individuals, so that fact-finding interviews can be focused on these individuals. In general, there are also some advantages to questionnaires. These are:

- They are relatively cheap to administer
- They are free of interviewer distortion and error
- They permit time to refer to documents and documentation, which may be particularly necessary where statistical data are requested
- It may be possible to ask more personal or controversial questions, especially if the respondent is permitted to remain anonymous.

Questionnaire design is a skilled activity, and the development of an appropriate questionnaire may take a considerable period of time. Several drafts, followed by pilot trials may be necessary before a questionnaire is ready to be used more widely. The questions on a questionnaire may be open-ended or closed or categorized questions. Categorized questions, which list the range of potential answers tend to reduce ambiguity and misinterpretation and are quicker to answer and analyse. In many ways, closed or categorized questions are to be preferred, but they do suffer from their dependence on the initial selection and expression of alternative answers. Open-ended questions are useful where the range of possible responses cannot readily be predicted, and can assist in collecting ideas, but their use does need to be carefully considered

Questionnaires – a checklist
1 Decide on the objectives of the questionnaire, i.e. what information is being collected, why is it wanted and how is it to be used?
2 Communicate these objectives to the user, via a brief introductory letter or notes at the beginning of the questionnaire.
3 Phrase the questions so that they are unambiguous, concise, unbiased, unoffensive (not leading) and free from jargon.
4 Arrange the questions in a logical and clearly structured order, grouping related questions together.
5 Keep the questionnaire as short as is consistent with the nature of the enquiry.
6 In designing the questionnaire, consider how the results are to be analysed, and arrange the questionnaire so that results can be input straight into a computer system.
7 Impose a deadline for response, and, if possible, include a prepaid addressed envelope for postal responses.

Analysing documents

Any system that is a candidate for computerization or for the introduction of a newer computer system is likely to generate documents. In a library acquisitions-and-ordering system documents recording the description of items to be acquired, invoices, statistics of new books acquired and associated documents will be generated. Each document in a system has its own cycle of creation, amendment, use and deletion. It may be useful to ascertain:

● What event triggers the generation of the document?
● Who generates the document?
● How is it prepared?
● Where are the data derived from?
● Who uses the document?
● For what purpose is it used?
● How is it stored?
● How long is it kept for?

Documents may also be copied or be multipart, with different copies going to different people and different departments. The purpose of each copy needs to be ascertained, and its filing sequence noted, as this usually indicates how copies are retrieved and used.

This analysis of existing documents can provide invaluable information about how the existing system works. The new system should not mirror the old system, but should improve upon it. In particular the analyst should seek to eliminate obsolescence and ambiguity and duplication of effort, and to offer additional system features as appropriate. Nevertheless an analysis of existing documents should reduce the likelihood of important functions being overlooked.

Recording documents

The National Computing Centre has produced a form on which a clerical-document specification may be recorded. Such a form prompts the analyst to seek further information, and to record that information in an organized and structured manner. Such a form may also be supplemented by various charts and grids. Such grids can reveal the way in which documents are processed and may uncover duplication. For example, a document/data item grid shows the duplication of data items on various documents. Document names are entered along the top of the grid and item names down the left-hand side. Marks are made in the grid where an item of data appears on a given document.

Observation

Observation of a system in operation can help to identify systems features that may not come to light by more structured methods of data gathering. Such features may not be formally documented or perceived as relevant by interviewees. The analyst can observe:

- Environmental conditions, such as level of noise, lighting
- Work conditions, such as extent of interruption, levels of super-vision and control, flow of work, normal and peak workloads
- Informal systems for producing and storing information such as personal data files, inter-office communication, methods for handling spontaneous 'one-off' enquiries
- Staff attitudes to work.

Observation is very time-consuming and its value depends on the skill of the observer. It is an activity that is difficult to structure, and which must be conducted differently in different circumstances. Care must be exercised, so that the analyst does not disturb the work patterns that he is trying to observe.

Special-purpose record keeping

Some information required by the analyst will not be available from interviews, or from existing documents. Typically, quantitative data concerning volumes, trends and frequencies may need to be specifically collected. In these cases it will be necessary to set up a special record-keeping exercise. Such records may be generated by the analyst, but are more likely to be created by staff as a by-product of their normal activities. Such record-generation exercises should be kept to a minimum, and any records that staff are requested to keep should require the minimum of effort and not interfere with their normal activities.

Systems-description techniques

All systems-description techniques are concerned with building models of existing and proposed systems. Models are aids to:

- Thinking
- Creativity
- Communication
- Testing potential performance.

In the use of any of the modelling techniques reviewed here, the following are important.

(a) *Simplicity*. All models are simplifications of the real world, where the essential or key features of the real-world systems have been identified. Systems models should convey the key features simply, without overlooking necessary details.

(b) *Consistency*. Symbols and terminology will be used to represent and describe aspects of information flow, organizational structure etc. These should be used consistently.

(c) *Completeness*. Models need to be complete in the areas that they cover, and not overlook essential processes or entities.

(d) *Precision*. Models must be accurate and precise.

(e) *Hierarchy*. Models must have some means of representing several levels of detail in the constructed models. In other words a number of models are likely to be necessary which can be fitted into a hierarchy of models.

The systems-description techniques that follow are useful in describing both current and proposed systems.

Organization charts

Organization charts are useful for recording organizational structures. They record the division of responsibilities and functions within an organization. Organizations can be structured in different ways.

Business organizations may be structured by:

- Location, e.g. geographical areas
- Customer type, e.g. commercial and private customers
- Product, e.g. metal tubes, bicycles, cookers
- Process, e.g. group of machines or plants
- Function, e.g. research, production, personnel.

Libraries may be structured according to:

- Function, e.g. lending or reference, children's and schools'
- Subject, e.g. science, social sciences
- Location, e.g. branch.

It is not uncommon to find a mixture of these divisions. This, together with the fact that organization charts may not reveal what is actually happening and who is really doing the work or shouldering responsibility, means that the analyst needs to appreciate both the formal and the informal organization structure. Organizations where the caretaker has more control over whether offices will open between Christmas and New Year than senior management are more common than one might suspect!

The organizational structure should be related to the organization's objectives. If, however, these objectives are unclear or have changed, the organizational structure may be less than effective. It is important for the analyst to have a firm grasp of the organizational structure, because it will determine communication links and contacts.

Activity charts
Activity charts can be useful in describing who does what activity. These take the form of a grid chart, with the people in a department listed down the left-hand side, and the activities listed across the top of the grid. Activity charts can be useful in identifying responsibility for specific tasks, and may give some indication of the man hours devoted to completing specified tasks.

Flow charts
A flowchart is a diagram composed of symbols, directional lines and other information which represents the way in which a computer will be used to solve a problem. It shows what is to be accomplished, rather than how it is to be accomplished. It is a useful tool for documenting information and document flow in the system. There are three main areas of application of flowcharts:

● During the investigation of existing sytems (as a means of recording findings)
● During the design of a system (to record a proposal)
● During the specification of a new system (to record operational procedures).

There are a number of different procedure flowcharting techniques, each with their own symbols. The symbols used in Figures 2.2 and 2.3 are the National Computing Centre (NCC) symbols, as recorded in BS 4058:1973. The symbols are used to represent data and operations. Symbols are joined by flowlines which show the order of events or flow of data. A flowchart has three main functions:

(a) To enable the systems analyst to be sure of completeness in the system specification, to identify any duplication, and to make it easier to compare specifications for changes
(b) To provide a basis for a clear and logical report or record of the system
(c) To provide a means of establishing communication with the people who will eventually operate the system.

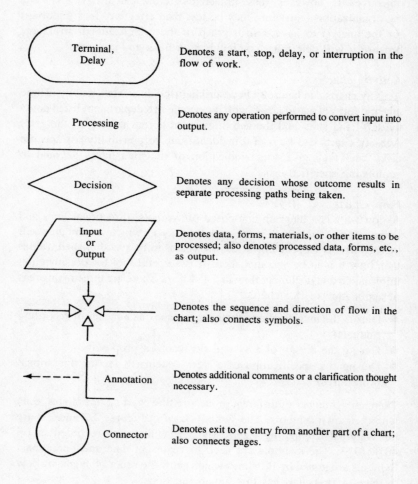

Terminal, Delay	Denotes a start, stop, delay, or interruption in the flow of work.
Processing	Denotes any operation performed to convert input into output.
Decision	Denotes any decision whose outcome results in separate processing paths being taken.
Input or Output	Denotes data, forms, materials, or other items to be processed; also denotes processed data, forms, etc., as output.
	Denotes the sequence and direction of flow in the chart; also connects symbols.
Annotation	Denotes additional comments or a clarification thought necessary.
Connector	Denotes exit to or entry from another part of a chart; also connects pages.

Fig. 2.2 Basic flowcharting symbols

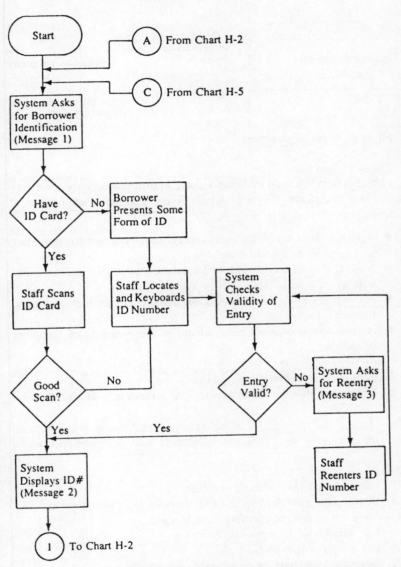

Fig. 2.3 A sample decision flowchart for part of an automated circulation system

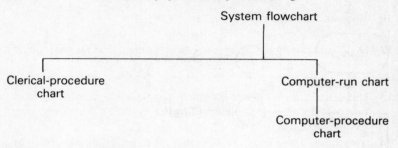

Fig. 2.4 Types of flowchart

Types of flowchart
Flowcharts can be used to depict a range of different activities and may function at different levels of detail. Figure 2.4 shows some types of flowchart:

- A *system flowchart* is the most general kind of flowchart, providing an overview of system functions
- A *clerical-procedure flowchart* depicts the user procedures associated with clerical activities
- A *computer-run chart* shows computer procedures such as inputs, files and outputs
- A *computer-procedure chart* identifies the elements of computer procedures.

Flowchart construction − a checklist
1 Remember that the basic structure of a flowchart should be:

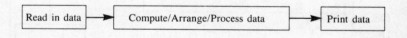

2 Use standard flowcharting symbols.
3 Develop the flowchart from top to bottom and show flows moving from top to bottom and from left to right.
4 Use arrowhead to represent direction.
5 Do not cross flowlines.
6 Keep the flowchart clear, readable and simple.
7 Break a complex problem into several flowcharts.
8 Leave space between symbols.
9 Write simple messages in flowchart symbols.

10 Be neat and legible.

11 Work at a consistent level of detail.

12 Don't join two incoming lines to one outgoing line at the same point, e.g.   not

13 Use connectors at top and bottom of page to allow continuing from one page to the next, although flowcharts should not extend over too many pages.

14 Tidy up all loose ends. For example, if there are three parts of an order form, all must arrive at a clearly defined end point.

15 Validate the flowchart by passing test data through.

A flowchart can be a useful means of recording the components of a system, but it also has limitations in this function. These are:

(a) It is difficult to write good flowcharts which avoid mixing levels of detail and do not become complex and untidy.

(b) It can be difficult to reproduce a flowchart.

(c) It can be difficult to trace backwards through a flowchart, and to identify the conditions that gave rise to a specific action.

(d) Flowcharts are difficult to amend without resorting to complete redrawing.

The above reasons, coupled with the fact that flowcharts and other techniques used by systems analysts are not always transparent to a user, have provoked a move towards systems-analysis-and-design methodologies that more closely model the user's perception of the real world. Flowcharts are now less extensively used than they once were, although they remain a useful tool.

Decision tables

Decision tables are a further charting technique that might be used in conjunction with flowcharts in order to examine specific detailed procedures. Decision tables are particularly appropriate to cover complex circumstances, where several criteria might determine an action. A decision table is a chart in which all of the actions to be performed under all combinations of conditions are defined. All of the actions to be taken when pre-specified conditions are fulfilled are defined. In order to explore decision tables further, it is necessary to define some of the components of a decision table.

● A *condition* is one of the factors that must be taken into account in deciding which procedure to follow.

- The *condition stub* is the collection of all relevant conditions.
- The *condition entry* is the combination of conditions which leads to a particular procedure.
- An *action* is one of the steps in a procedure.
- The *action stub* is the collection of all actions involved in a procedure.
- The *action entry* is the combination of actions which belongs to a procedure.
- A *rule* is the combination of conditions which leads to a particular set of actions.

The format of a decision table is shown in Figure 2.5(a). Decision tables are useful in checking that all combinations and conditions have been taken into account, and facilitate the comparison and analysis of various combinations. They can be directly input into the computer, with the aid of decision-table processors and pre-processors. They are more concise than flowcharts in documenting procedures in which several complex decisions have to be made.

There are three different kinds of decision tables: limited-entry tables, extended-entry tables, and mixed-entry tables. The simplest of these is the limited-entry table. (For an example, see Figure 2.5(b).) In a limited-entry table all conditions are expressed as either Y (they do apply) or N (they do not apply) and all actions are performed (X) or not performed ($-$). The statement of each action is completely contained in the appropriate stub, or limited to that stub.

	RULES R_1; R_2; R_3; R_N
CONDITION STUB	CONDITION ENTRIES
ACTION STUB	ACTION ENTRIES

Fig. 2.5(a)   The format of a decision table

Conditions	Rules				
	1	2	3	4	5
Did the system cost more than £10,000?	Y	Y	Y	N	N
Is continuous operation of the system vital?	N	N	Y	N	Y
Can operating staff deal with minor technical problems?	N	Y	N	Y	Y

Actions

Employ technician			X		
Monthly systems overhaul	X	X			
Call-out on demand	X				X
Call-out on 24 hours' notice			X	X	

Fig. 2.5(b) An example of a limited-entry decision table for selecting systems-maintenance arrangements

Decision-table construction — a checklist
1 Start by working out the various conditions and write them in the condition stub, with the most significant one first. If more than four conditions apply, divide the table into two or more tables.
2 Identify all the actions and record them in the action stub in the sequence in which they occur.
3 Draw up all the rules for desired combinations of conditions. For a limited-entry table, if there are n conditions, there will be 2n rules.
4 Record the appropriate action for each condition.
5 Check for ambiguity, or the same combinations of conditions giving different actions.
6 Check the table for redundancy, or the same action caused by different rules or combinations of conditions.
7 Check the table for accuracy and completeness.
8 Use a top-down hierarchy of tables where more than one table is necessary, because there are too many conditions operating to result in a simple table.

Decision trees

Decision trees are another way of showing the alternative actions that can result from different combinations of circumstances. The tree is read from left to right, with the actions to be taken recorded down the right-hand side of the diagram (see Figure 2.6).

Decision trees are most appropriate for logic verification of moderately complex decisions which result in up to 10−15 actions. They are useful for presenting the logic of a decision table to users.

Tight or structured English

Narrative accounts can be more carefully structured and made less ambiguous by the use of tight or structured English. Structured English uses standard narrative constructs to constrain the language. On the other hand, since concepts are essentially presented in English, the narrative should be easily comprehensible.

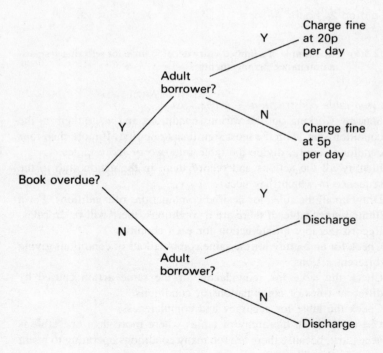

Fig. 2.6 A decision tree

The basic constraints of Structured English are:

(a) Sequences of events or actions are described simply by using the top to bottom order of the statements. The following actions, for example, are undertaken in the order presented:

> For all orders
> > Calculate value
> > If value exceeds £100
> > Delete order
> > List orders by Department

(b) Circumstances where actions depend upon differing conditions can be described using conditional statements such as IF........ELSE ....ENDIF; e.g.:

> IF the book is reserved
> > Shelve in reserved section
> > Create notification
> ELSE (the book is not reserved)
> > Reshelve in normal sequence

(c) When one of several possible cases apply, statements can be used such as:

	Terms of payment
CASE 1	For each order
CASE 2	Examine credit limit
or	CASE 1 Credit limit £1000
WHEN .... DO	CASE 2 Credit limit £5000
WHEN .... DO	CASE 3 Credit limit unlimited
	ENDCASE

(d) Repetition of action can be described using statements such as:

> DO WHILE .... ENDWHILE,
> or   DO UNTIL .... ENDUNTIL,
> or   FOR ALL ....; e.g.

> DO WHILE records on file
> > IF a claim in last year
> > > IF over 25
> > > > add 100 to PREMIUM
> > > ELSE (less than 25)
> > > > add 200 to PREMIUM
> > END-IF

```
      ELSE (no claim in last year)
      IF over 25
         add 10 to PREMIUM
      ELSE (less than 25)
         add 25 to PREMIUM
      END-IF

   END-IF
      Print NAME and ADDRESS
      Print PREMIUM

   ENDWHILE
```

The hierarchy of constructs is shown by indentation. Structured English is most useful wherever the problem involves combining sequences of actions with decisions and loops.

Logical modelling

Introduction
The techniques considered in the previous section are useful for describing existing systems and to some extent for describing proposed systems. Some of them, however, tend to incorporate the organizational structure of the existing system. Logical modelling techniques, on the other hand, encourage the development of a logical model that shows the information-processing requirements of an organization, independently of the current organizational structure.

Computerized systems are prone to reflect the characteristics of the manual system they replace. In an office, for example, certain functions or jobs may no longer be necessary in a computerized system. It can be difficult to identify and recognize these functions. For a variety of reasons online public-access catalogues in libraries are essentially computerized card catalogues. It is important to identify the logical components of a system, if there is to be any likelihood of a complete re-appraisal of the information-processing system.

Establishment of a logical model of requirements should proceed independently of external constraints. Once an ideal or 'target' model has been developed, a model of 'what is possible' may be evolved. This model should be reviewed from time to time in the light of the changing environment with the objective of moving the actual model closer to the ideal model. Dataflow diagrams show the passage of data through a system, and focus on the logical events required by the system.

Dataflow diagrams

Dataflow diagrams (DFDs) are central to most structured systems-analysis-and-design methodologies. The notation varies between methodologies: here we use the National Computing Centre symbols. All DFDs are graphical, and it is intended that they be amenable to non-computer specialist users. DFDs can be used both to show current physical activities and for the logical model of the system. Here we are emphasizing their use in this second context.

Basic DFD symbols

- A *dataflow* is a route which enables packets of data to travel from one point to another. Data may flow from a source to a process, or to and from a data store or process. The flow is depicted by an arrowed line, with the arrowhead pointing in the direction of flow. Dataflows should be named with names that clearly describe the flows, and which are unique. Dataflows moving in and out of stores do not need names, the store name serves to describe them.
- A *process* represents a transformation, where incoming dataflows are changed into outgoing dataflows. Processes must also have clear, informative names. Appropriate labels often include an active verb (e.g. compute, retrieve, store, verify), followed by an object or object class.
- A *data store* is a repository of data such as a database file or a card index. Stores, again, should have clear names. If a process merely uses the contents of a store and does not alter it the arrowhead goes only from the store to the process. If the details in the store are altered by the process, then a double-headed arrow is used.
- A *source or sink* is a person or part of an organization which enters or receives data from the system but is considered to be outside the context of the dataflow model. Sources and sinks force useful consideration of the boundaries of the system.
- A *physical flow* shows the flow of material.

Figure 2.7(a) shows the basic DFD symbols and (b) gives examples of two simple DFDs from a video library.

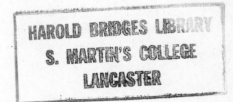

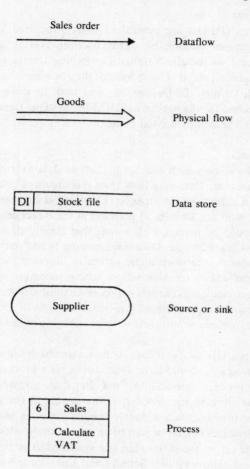

Fig. 2.7(a)   Basic dataflow diagram symbols

Based on: Downs, E. and others, *Structured systems analysis and design method: application and context*, London, Prentice-Hall, 1988.

Level 1, Video library

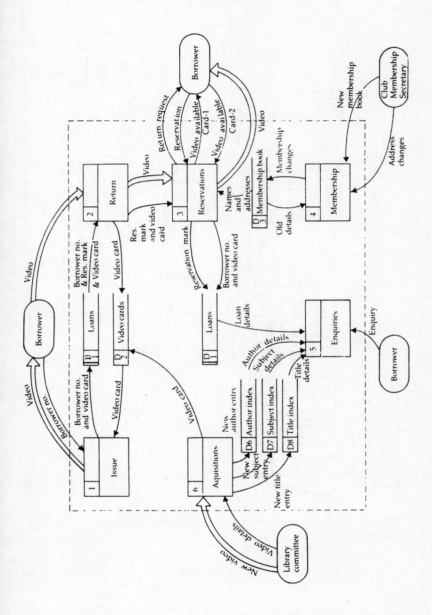

Fig. 2.7(b) Sample dataflow diagrams

Level 2, Video library reservations

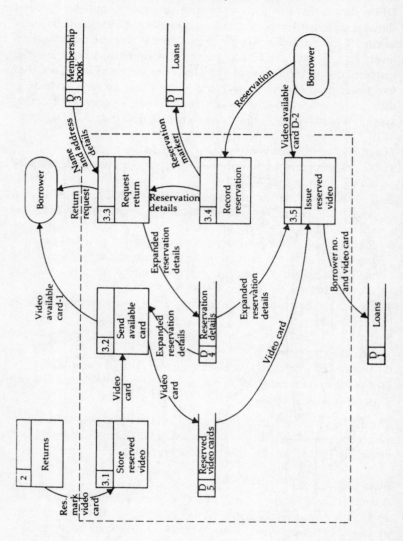

Fig. 2.7(b) (continued)

Hierarchies
DFDs should be used in a hierarchical structure to represent models showing different levels of detail. The top-level DFD, conventionally labelled 0, can be used to give a system overview, whereas the subsequent levels 1, 2, 3, etc. can be used to show more detailed aspects of the system. The numbering system of the level 0 model needs to be continued into lower-level diagrams, so that they can easily be referred back to their parent processes. This is achieved by using a decimal numbering system. Thus process 3 may be decomposed into 3.1, 3.2, 3.3, etc.

Dataflow diagram construction − a checklist
1 Attempt to grasp central principles, rather than being confused by detail.
2 Try to identify sinks and sources. This will both provide system boundaries and identify a set of dataflows related to the sinks and sources.
3 Starting with this input from a source or output to a sink, place a box where a process is required to transform the dataflow. Review the data needs of the process, and, accordingly, identify additional data items.
4 Accept the need to re-draft the diagram several (probably at least three) times.
5 Follow a typical transaction through the system, modelling the logical activities that affect it.
6 Remember that most processes access a store of some kind.
7 Do not strive for absolute correctness. There is often more than one way to draw a DFD.

The DFD provides a clear impression of how data pass through the system, but it fails to represent the passage in sufficient detail for systems design. A data dictionary can be a useful tool in this context.

Data dictionaries
A data dictionary is simply a dictionary of data. It is a collection of data about data known as metadata. It may be compiled on sheets of paper or stored in a computer database. Dataflow diagrams can be used to document the flow of data through an information system, and define relationships between processes, dataflows and data stores, but do not actually define these themselves. This is the role of the data dictionary. The data dictionary holds information concerning:

● Stores
● Processes

- Flows
- Data elements
- Data structures.

Stores, processes and flows have already been introduced in the previous section.

- A *data element* is an item of data which has been decomposed as far as is appropriate for the task in hand. Precisely what constitutes a data element will vary from one system to another. A data element is a named item of data which cannot be decomposed into any other logically meaningful data items. Examples might be a borrower's name or a department name.
- A *data structure* is a collection of data elements that regularly appear together. Thus a data structure can be used as a shorthand reference in flow, process and store definitions. Any group of data that has been named will be defined as a data structure. Examples might be invoice, reservation, etc.

The structure of the entry for the various components will vary. Typically entries for each of the components include:

Data element
- Name − a meaningful unique name
- Description − of the data element
- Aliases − alternative terms used for the same data element by different people or within different contexts
- Type − i.e. whether it is character, numeric or alphanumeric
- Format
- Values − range of values that the element may take
- Security − who is allowed to modify, add or delete a given data item
- Editing − concerning the way in which data are produced from the system
- Comments − any special information.

Data structure
- Name
- Description
- A list of associated elements and structures which are documented elsewhere in the dictionary
- Volume information
- Comments.

Data store
- Name
- Description
- Dataflows in
- Contents — may well be described in terms of data structures which reveal the interrelationships in the system
- Dataflows out
- Physical organization
- Comments.

Dataflow
- Name
- Source reference and description given using the reference numbers allocated to the process in the dataflow diagram
- Destination reference and description
- Dataflow description
- Content
- Volume information
- Comments.

Dataflow entries define input and output requirements and help to determine the content of forms and reports as well as contributing to decisions concerning input and output technology.

Data process
- Name
- Description
- Inputs
- Logic
- Output
- Comments
- Reference (full logic description).

The logic of a process may be documented with a variety of tools, such as decision tables, decision trees and structured English. Process entries form the basis of clerical-procedure documents and computer programs.

The data dictionary is a central source in logical systems definition. The dictionary is dynamic, and is built up as the analyst learns more about the system. The data dictionary supports a complex web of interrelationships. A single data element may appear in many data structures, dataflows, data stores and processes. When an element is amended, the implications of the amendment must be traced through the various structures, flows and stores and processes. Data dictionary software or systems (DDS) can support this process.

Data dictionaries have become more important as organizations have recognized the importance of data as a resource. Data dictionaries and the software that can be used to compile them can be used to support most analysis and design activities. In general they may assist management in:

● Maintaining control over what data exist and how they are used
● Controlling modifications to existing data or processes using data
● Controlling plans for new users of data and the acquisition of new types of data.

The following list of application areas for data dictionaries taken from Leong-Hong and Plagman encompasses most aspects of systems analysis and design:

● Systems planning
● Requirements definition and analysis
● Design
● Implementation, programming, testing and conversion
● Documentation and standards
● Operational control and audit trail
● End-user support.

The data dictionaries should function at two distinct levels: the logical level and the implementation level.

1   The *logical level* analyses the requirements, irrespective of how they are to be met. It is a model of the organization, and should record details of:

● Entities and relationships of concern to the enterprise
● Processes of interest to the enterprise
● Responsibility for processes
● Flows resulting from processes, external entities or events
● Connections that exist between entities, processes and events.

2   The *implementation level* records physical-design decisions in terms of the implemented database or file structures and the programs that access them. It helps to establish the design of the system, to prove its correctness and to identify the impact and cost of changes. It clearly must be logically consistent with the logical model, and match it in scope. Examples of the kind of data that should be recorded include:

● *Data-description elements* which describe the different data types and structures used in the systems, such as records and files

- *Process-description elements* which describe the processes in the system
- Details of *physical storage* of data and its use.

The data-dictionary software should also validate for syntax, consistency and completeness, offering checks on, for example:

- Characteristics of each physical file
- The contents of each file
- Each physical structure.

The implementation level must contain all the information necessary to derive an optimum operational schedule. This is supported by the collection of performance and utilization statistics on file use, such as frequency of access, response times, when a file is assessed, by whom and what for. These data may help in arriving at a database or file structure that gives optimum performance.

Function of a data dictionary
Data dictionaries are used in:

- *Consistency checking*, for example in a dataflow diagram, where such checking can ensure that all flows have sources and destinations, all data elements in stores have a means of arriving in the store etc.
- *Testing*: data descriptions and ranges of values can allow test data to be automatically generated.
- *Coding*: the description of data structures may be sufficient to support the generation of data descriptions in the host language or data manipulation language (DML) through a pre-compilation pass of the dictionary.
- *Change*: data dictionaries are invaluable in tracing the effects of change through a complete system.

Entity life-histories

Entity life-histories (ELHs) provide an additional perspective on the data in a system, by providing a means of representing how entities change within a system with the passage of time. ELHs start with the creation of an entity, record the sequence of changes which take place during its life within the system and end with its removal from the system. ELHs can be used alongside DFDs and other data-analysis techniques to validate their completeness and correctness. Since ELHs specify priority and sequence, they regulate the manner in which a system runs.

ELHs are used to help define the logic associated with update processes. Three basic concepts need first to be defined:

(a) *Update processes* are processes which result in changes to the systems data. This update processing can be represented as in Figure 2.8(a) and (b). The diamond shapes represent tests which are performed within the process. In this case they test the validity of the incoming data by checking their format and determining whether an entity occurrence for the new staff member has already been created. The creation of the entity for the new staff member is an effect, and the receipt within the system of the input dataflow 'new details' is a trigger or event which activates the process 'add to file'. In general, an *update process* results from an *event* and incorporates the *tests* and conditions to cause *effects*. This provides us with the two other concepts:

(b) *Events* activate update processes. They may take the form of an input dataflow or a notification to the system that a particular point in time has been reached.

(c) *Effects* are the outcomes of a process. They may be the creation or deletion of entity occurrences, changes to the attributes of entity occurrences, the creation or deletion of relationships, or a combination of the above.

(a) *As represented on a DFD*

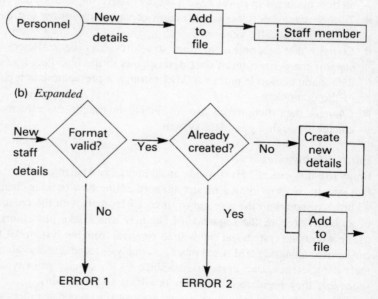

(b) *Expanded*

Fig. 2.8 **An update process**

General structure of ELHs

The general structure of an ELH is indicated in Figures 2.9 and 2.10. Note that the events follow the sequence 'create', 'amend', 'delete' as exemplified in Figures 2.9 and 2.10.

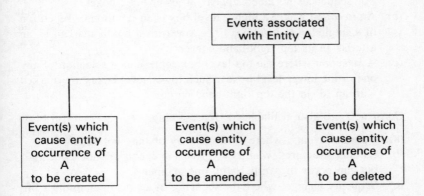

Fig. 2.9 General structure of an entity life-history

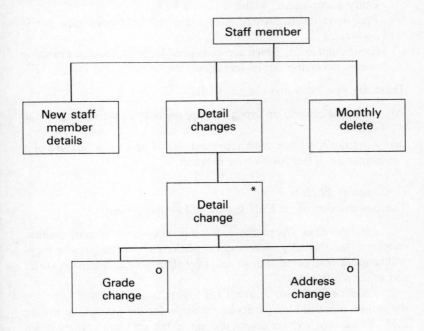

Fig. 2.10 An example of a simple entity life-history

A box on an ELH with lower-level boxes represents one of:

(a) A *sequence* will be represented by a series of lower-level boxes reading from left to right, thus in Figure 2.10, 'New staff member details' precedes 'Detail changes', which precedes 'Monthly delete'. For sequences no labels appear in lower-level boxes.

(b) An *iteration* where a higher-level box is an iteration or repetition of a single lower-level box. The lower-level box is marked by an asterisk in its top right-hand corner.

(c) A *selection* where the top-level box represents a selection of any one of the lower-level boxes. Such lower-level boxes are marked with an 'o' in the top right-hand corner.

Constructs are also available for representing:

(a) Optional events, where an event may or may not occur

(b) Parallel structures, where two groups of events are not sequential, but can occur in parallel with one another

(c) Sequence change, where the sequence of events in an entity's life changes

(d) Events which have more than one simultaneous effect on different entity occurrences, within a simple ELH

(e) Premature deaths, where entities are deleted before their life is completed

(f) Error conditions, which are associated with unexpected events or events occurring out of sequence.

There are two rules that control ELHs:

(a) An event causing an effect can appear only at the bottom of the structure

(b) A higher-level box must represent *one* of and not a mixture of a sequence, a selection or an iteration.

Constructing ELHs

The construction of an ELH should follow these steps:

1 *Identify events.* In order to do this it is necessary to identify entities, relationships, attributes, events and conditions. Consultation with users will be useful, but some of these data may already be embodied in DFDs and other models.

2 *Produce ELH matrix.* The ELH matrix is a grid which identifies the entities affected by a particular event, as for the example in Figure 2.11. Events are written across the top of the grid and entities down the side.

Event

Entity	1	2	3	4	5	6
A	I					D
B		I		M	I	
C		M			M	
D				D	I	
E		D	I			

Fig. 2.11 An entity life-history matrix

Entries in the grid follow:

I = Insert
M = Modify
D = Delete

Checking of the grid should ensure that every event affects at least one entity, and that every entity has an event which creates it.

3 *Draw initial ELHs*. Draw an initial ELH for each entity. The steps in achieving this are:

- Identify events that cause the creation of an entity
- Identify the events that cause the amendment of an entity, and decide upon their sequence
- Build a structure, probably working from the 'bottom up'
- Add deletion events
- Check and look for further events.

4 *Review ELHs*. Consider all master/detail relationships, taking a 'top—down' view. The ELH matrix should be checked and additional events incorporated. Events should be checked to ensure that they can be recognized by the system. The same qualified event should not appear more than once in an ELH.

5 *Produce event catalogue*. The event catalogue is a catalogue which names and describes events.

Entity life-histories can be used as both an analysis and a design tool. They may be used in conjunction with dataflow diagrams and other entity—relationship models.

Conclusion
This chapter has introduced the concept of a methodology for systems

analysis, and reviewed a range of techniques that may be applied during systems analysis. Clearly, the most appropriate technique will depend upon circumstances. These techniques together offer approaches for collecting, describing and analysing data about systems. They may be applied to an existing system in order to assess its operation, effectiveness and efficiency, or they may be used to gather information relating to the requirements for a new system.

The analysis phase of a project should conclude with a systems specification. This specification should record and interpret the data collected and organized by the techniques covered in this chapter. It is likely, therefore, that whilst some of the specification will take the form of text, some of it must be in the form of charts, diagrams and tables.

The techniques outlined in this chapter may be used within the framework of a structured approach to analysis. This structured approach makes a distinction between analysis and design and produces a specification which is:

- *Graphic*, whose main components are dataflow diagrams and other graphic devices
- *Partitioned and top-down*, so that the reader can absorb both a general view and more detailed views of the system
- *Iterative*, such that small sections can be studied by user and analyst
- *Easily maintained*, because it is partitioned
- *Easily understandable*, because it concentrates on the logical aspects of the system
- *A logical model* of the system with minimal reference to physical details, so that the specification and any consequent design is not constrained by existing technology
- *Precise and concise.*

Further reading

Central Computer and Telecommunications Agency, *Operational Requirement (OR)*, London, CCTA, 1982 (Computer Circular 137).

Daniels, A. and Yeates, D., *Basic systems analysis*, 2nd edn., London, Pitman, 1984.

Davis, G. B., 'Strategies for information requirements determination', *IBM systems journal*, **21** (1), 1982, 4−30.

Downs, E. and others, *Structured systems analysis and design method: application and content*, London, Prentice-Hall, 1988.

Thomas, P. A., *Task analysis of library operations*, London, Aslib, 1971 (Aslib occasional publications 8).

Wroe, B. and Skidmore, S., *Structured systems analysis*, Manchester, National Computing Centre Publications, 1988.

Chapter Three

Database design

Introduction

This chapter considers some of the key facets of database design. Since many library and information applications involve the creation and maintenance of databases, it is important that the information professional appreciates the techniques and approaches used in database design. In some microcomputer systems the information professional may be responsible for the design of the database. In larger systems some of the aspects of database design may be already determined by the system, and their control may be beyond the scope of the information professional. Nevertheless, to participate fully in the development of effective database applications it is necessary to appreciate the fundamental concepts that are encountered in this area.

Databases

- A *database* is a generalized integrated collection of data together with its description, which is managed in such a way that it can fulfil the differing needs of its users.
- A *database-management system* (DBMS) is a system that generates, runs and maintains databases, and as such the system must include all of the software needed for this purpose.
- A *data model* specifies the rules according to which data are structured and also the associated operations that are permitted. It may also be viewed as a technique for the formal description of data, data relationships and usage constraints.

The database concept emerged in the late 1960s as users' demand for more information coincided with advances in computer technology and increased expertise in software engineering. Traditional file-based systems were found to be inadequate, particularly for generating high-level planning and control information which relates to the whole organization. The generation of this kind of information requires the organization's data to be viewed as a single unit and not as a set of independent units stored in separate files. Figure 3.1 compares (a) the traditional file approach with (b) the database approach for a simplified example of a library circulation-control system.

(a)   *Traditional file approach*

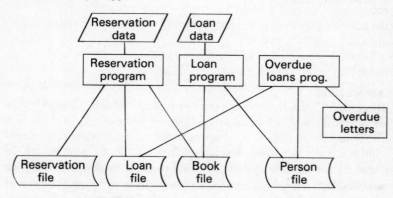

(b)   *Database approach*

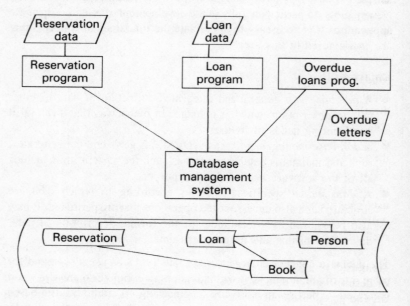

Fig. 3.1   A library circulation-control system

Although the database will probably be stored physically as a set of files, users and applications do not need to know anything about the physical storage. Stored with the actual data is a description of the database, which enables the database-management system to retrieve information from the database, to store new data in appropriate places in the database, establishing relationships with other data if relevant. The applications do not directly access the database; instead they pass requests to the database system to retrieve or store data. In essence, then, the traditional file approach is program-oriented, whereas the database approach is data-oriented.

This shift towards data orientation has placed much importance on data modelling and database design.

Whilst the database approach is generally to be strived towards, there are circumstances in which to organize all of an organization's data into one database is not feasible, either for a variety of economic, political or organizational reasons or merely because the data are too complex to be modelled in a single database. There are also some disadvantages to the database approach:

- *Complexity.* The DBMS is a complex piece of software and database and application design needs care and time.
- *Cost.* Comprehensive DBMSs are expensive and may incur over-heads in terms of processing time and storage space.
- *Inefficiencies* in processing may arise, with unexpected or changed database-usage patterns.

Models

Figure 3.2 summarizes the standard data-model architecture. The different levels in this model give different *views* of the database. The conceptual model is central in that it provides a logical view of the complete database. The conceptual model identifies those elements of the real-world information that are relevant to particular applications.

At the top level, the user views or external views represent sub-sets of the conceptual model. There may be many different application or user views of the system. At the bottom level, the physical-storage view will be represented in terms of file names, file organizations, access methods etc.

These models fit into the overall *architecture* of a database system. As in Figure 3.3 in place of models there are corresponding schemas, or descriptions of data models. The language used for the schema will depend upon the actual DBMS used. Normally the DBMS will draw on all schemas to support the applications. In schema updates arrows may

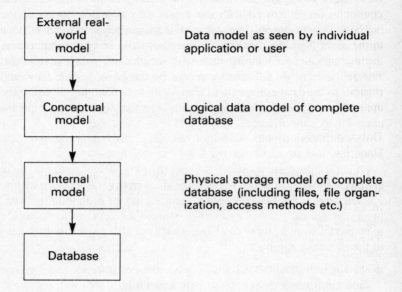

Fig. 3.2 Different levels of data model

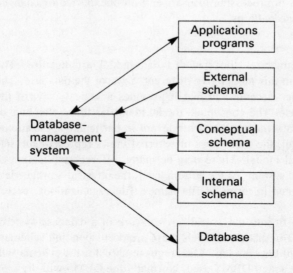

Fig. 3.3 Architecture of a typical database system

represent data travelling in the opposite direction, i.e. from the DBMS to conceptual, external or internal schema. Note that the applications communicate with the DBMS and reference external schema only.

The DBMS performs the mapping from items in the external schema to the associated items in the conceptual schema and hence references the internal schema for information about the physical storage of the items referred to. The DBMS also accesses the database itself to store and retrieve data and communicates the results of the database access to the applications.

Database development

Database development involves the following five stages:

1 *Data investigation.* This involves the identification of the nature and use of data, using some of the approaches and techniques discussed in Chapter Two. All facts gathered at the data-investigation stage represent data about data, often referred to as *metadata*. Clearly such data need to be stored and organized for easy access. The product of such organization will be a *data dictionary*. Data dictionaries were discussed more fully in Chapter Two.

2 *Data modelling* is the process that will lead to a conceptual model of the real-world concepts. This is a generalized model, in that it is independent of any specific DBMS.

3 *Database design* involves mapping the conceptual model into a DBMS-specific data model. The end result of the process will be a DBMS-specific conceptual schema and external schema. The conceptual schema is the description of the database written in the data-description language (DDL) provided by the DBMS. External schemas are descriptions of the individual user and applications views.

4 *Database implementation.* At this stage the internal or storage schema will be created, with reference to the DBMS data model. Decisions need to be made concerning physical database characteristics, such as file sizes, file organization, access methods, and other physical aspects not fixed by the DBMS. The final phase of the stage is the creation of the actual database.

5 *Database monitoring and tuning.* Like all other aspects of the system, once the database is in operation it should be subject to regular monitoring in order to detect any inefficiencies, errors or omissions. Tuning will then be necessary to improve the situation. This tuning should not interfere with the user applications. In the longer term monitoring may highlight the need for redevelopment of databases to cater for changes in the environment.

Data modelling

Databases are created so that the data within them may be used. The data will be extracted from the database as a result of scheduled or on-demand enquiries. It is important that the database is organized in such a way that all enquiries can be met within the specified time and cost constraints. Users are not concerned with how the processing works, but merely that it does work. User requirements in respect of enquiries to the system and the responses they expect have a fundamental influence on database design. There are however four main problems in defining database requirements:

● Users may find it difficult to be sufficiently precise in specifying the form of enquiries and responses
● Users may have difficulty in raising their perceptions above those of the present system, to the potential of a new system
● Users are not aware of the time, space, and financial trade-offs associated with the retrieval of data
● Different users have different requirements. They may need different data, or the same data presented differently. They have different views of the real world.

Nevertheless it is clear that to fulfil differing user requirements and to incorporate a range of user models of the real world a database has to use flexible data and storage structures. The flexibility is achieved by structuring data along their natural data relationships.

Data analysis can assist in examining, understanding and modelling the logical structure of the data that an organization uses. Data analysis is complementary to the logical modelling of processes such as is achieved in dataflow diagrams. Data analysis aims to build a data model that supports, but is not driven by, the identified processes.

Systematic data analysis leads to:

● A better understanding of the logical data structure, which leads to better design and more flexible systems
● Identification of data structures. These are often more stable than a user's functional requirements or organizational structure, and are thus more fundamental
● An improved user understanding and evaluation of data models
● An increased likelihood of satisfactory shared-data systems, with greater control over data security and integrity and less duplication. of stored data.

A variety of different methodologies for data modelling have been proposed. Only two methods of data modelling are introduced here:

entity — relationship modelling and normalization of data tables.

All data modelling needs to identify the entities and attitudes relevant to a situation and the relationships between them. These are first defined and introduced in the context of entity — relationship modelling.

Entity — relationship modelling

Entity — relationship modelling is a technique for analysing and modelling an organization's data requirements. It requires the discovery of the data elements needed to support the information system and represents their structure in a clear, concise diagram. The basic concepts of entity — relationship modelling are:

(a) *Entity*: something about which it is desirable to store data. An entity must be uniquely defined, but may vary from a physical object (such as a 'book') to a more abstract concept, such as a 'sales area'.

(b) *Attribute*: a property or characteristic of an entity. For example, the entity 'book' may have the attributes 'title', 'author' and 'date of publication'.

(c) *Relationship*: relationships link entities. So, for example, the entity 'supplier' may be associated with the entity 'order' by a relationship that might be called 'placed with'. The entity 'book' may be linked to the entity 'title' by the relationship 'is named'.

Entity — relationship modelling highlights the entities that are important to the organizations and summarizes the relationships that exist between these entities.

Before proceeding to examine how these concepts can be incorporated into modelling techniques, it is useful also to note that:

● Entity — relationship modelling is difficult to perform, until the problem is well understood.

● Entities and attributes are not absolute; they depend on the system under consideration.

● An entity normally needs more than one attribute to be an entity

● Distinctions must be made between *entity type* and *entity occurrence*. For example the entity type may be 'book', but the entity occurrence is a specific book.

● An entity must be capable of being *uniquely identified*. In order that this be possible there must be an identifying attribute or combination of attributes which are termed the entity *identifier*. Any attribute could potentially operate as the entity identifier, but it must be chosen so that it can uniquely identify an entity occurrence. For example, borrower number is more satisfactory than borrower name, since a library may have more than one borrower with the same name. In most systems it is necessary to introduce a code to guarantee uniqueness. Such a code is the ISBN number for books. If more than one potential unique identifier exists then the identifier's stability and brevity may be considered in selecting the appropriate identifier.

Drawing entity—relationship diagrams

The construction of entity—relationship diagrams involves the following stages:

1   The *identification of important entities* and the relationships between them. These may emerge in dataflow diagrams, data dictionaries, and other earlier stages of the study.

2   The *interaction of entities via relationships* can be illustrated by examples of entity occurrences of Borrowers, Loans and Books and the relationships between them, in the form of an *entity—relationship occurrence diagram*, for example Figure 3.4.

3   A more concise picture is given in an *entity—relationship* diagram, for example Figure 3.5. In this diagram rectangles are used to display entities and relationships are described within diamond-shaped boxes. Connecting lines show which entities are associated with which relationship.

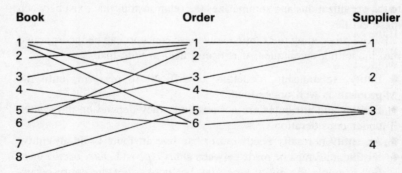

Fig. 3.4   Entity—relationship occurrence diagram

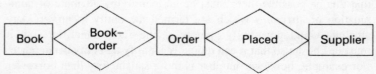

Fig. 3.5   Entity—relationship diagram

The *degree of a relationship* is an important property of a relationship. Relationships may be 1:N (one-to-many) or M:N (many-to-many). A 1:N relationship is one where the relationship occurrences fan out in one direction only. For example, the relationship between order and supplier is many-to-one or M:1, in that a given order can be placed with only one supplier, yet a supplier may receive many orders.

In a M:N relationship several relationship occurrences fan out in both directions, to link, for example, many 'book' entities to many 'order' entities. Thus an order may include several books, whilst a book may also be itemized on several orders.

1:N and M:N relationships can be shown on the lines connecting the entity symbols on the entity—relationship diagram, as in Figure 3.6. Such a relationship expresses the rules of the organization.

4   Entities and relationships need *labels or names*. Entities often have fairly obvious names, but relationships may present more of a problem. One useful solution is to construct a name that is a combination of the names of associated entities (e.g. book—order).

The notation in an entity—relationship diagram which shows the degree of relationship codifies the rules of the organization. For example, in the diagram in Figure 3.6 the rules of the situation are:

- Several books may be included on one order
- A supplier may receive many orders
- An order may be submitted to only one supplier.

If the entity—relationship diagram were modified to that in Figure 3.7, where the 'book' to 'order' relationship is 1:N, then any given book would be allowed to be ordered on only one order.

More detail
Having established the basic structure of the entity—relationship model, it is necessary to discover other necessary *attributes* and assign each to an entity. Data elements in the data dictionary provide a major source of attributes.

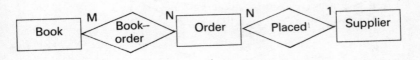

Fig. 3.6 Entity—relationship diagram showing degree of relationship

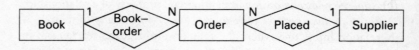

Fig. 3.7 Modified entity – relationship diagram

Some attributes can be clearly assigned to entities. For example supplier name and supplier address may be assigned to 'supplier', whilst the attributes title and price logically belong to the entity 'book'. But other attributes can be less clearly assigned. For example quantity ordered does not easily fit with 'order', 'book' or 'supplier'.

These attributes may be allocated by decomposing many-to-many relationships. This can be achieved by regarding the many-to-many relationship, such as 'Book – order', as a separate entity, and allocating attributes, such as quantity ordered to this new entity.

In general, many-to-many relationships should be decomposed into two 1:N relationships in order to clarify the entity – relationship model. Also, many database-management systems do not support many-to-many relationships and so these relationships must be decomposed into two 1:N relationships before they can be mapped on to the software.

In our example, this can be achieved by treating the relationship Book – order as a separate entity. This entity could be called 'Book – order' but more appropriately may be renamed 'One book – order', since it is concerned with the component of an order that relates to one individual book. Quantity ordered could now be placed against the new entity 'One book – order'. Figure 3.8 shows how the use of 'One book – order' as an entity serves to decompose the M:N relationship into two 1:N relationships.

(a) *Entity – relationship occurrence diagram*

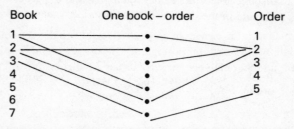

Fig. 3.8 Entity – relationship diagrams showing the 'Book – order' relationship replaced by a 'One book – order' entity

(b) *Entity—relationship diagram*

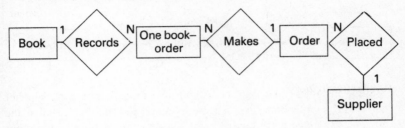

Fig. 3.8 (cont.)

1:1 relationships may also occur. For example a new entity 'Supplier—detail' could be related to 'Supplier' by a 1:1 relationship. 'Supplier detail' could contain additional elements of details concerning suppliers such as average delivery time, stock size etc. This would find expression in the following rule:

a 'Supplier' may have, at most, one 'Supplier—detail';
a 'Supplier—detail' may belong to, at most, one 'Supplier'.

Membership class or domain is concerned with how the nature of the relationship is affected by obligatory and non-obligatory rules found in the problem under investigation. Each entity and attribute is a member of a set of objects of a particular type; that is, each one belongs to a particular class or domain. This can be represented by the type of diagram in Figure 3.9. A blob inside the entity symbol (as in (a)) signifies that the entity's membership class or domain is obligatory, whereas a blob outside the entity symbol (as in (b)) means that it is not obligatory.

Figure 3.9(a) signifies that a book must have at least one publisher, and a publisher must have at least one stocked book, whereas (b) signifies that a book need not have a publisher, and a publisher need not have published a stocked book.

In a similar manner, diagrams may be drafted to show obligatory/non-obligatory relationships and non-obligatory/obligatory relationships. Recognition of membership classes can assist in the design of file structures.

Summary of the stages of entity—relationships modelling
The stages in data modelling using entity—relationships modelling can then be summarized as:

(a) *Obligatory*

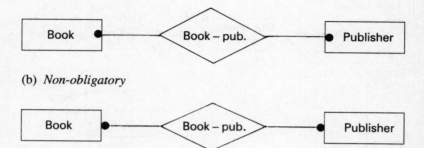

(b) *Non-obligatory*

Fig. 3.9 Membership classes

1 Identify entities and relationships between them.
2 Identify attributes associated with entities.
3 Determine whether any attributes are associated with relationships, and where necessary create relationship sets from these relationships.
4 Select identifiers for each entity set.
5 Determine the domain or class from which each attribute is drawn.
6 Produce an integrated data-model diagram.

This data-modelling approach is described as a top-down approach in that it involves identifying the main entities in the system, defining relationships between them, and assigning attributes to entities.

Normalization

Normalization is another widely used data-modelling approach and can be regarded as a bottom-up approach. Normalization was originally devised as a database-design tool for relational databases, but can also be used for conceptual modelling for other types of databases. Relational databases are discussed in the next section.

Normalization involves the analysis of functional dependencies between attributes (or data items). The purpose of normalization is to produce a set of small, stable data structures, with relationships being represented by replication of data items. Normalization ensures that insertions, deletions and amendments may then be made to the data without undesirable consequences. The basic steps in normalization are shown in Figure 3.10. In the first normal form, data aggregates are removed, by breaking the unnormalized relation into a number of other relations. The second and third normal forms remove partial and indirect dependencies of attributes on candidate keys. At each stage, the relation is broken down into several others.

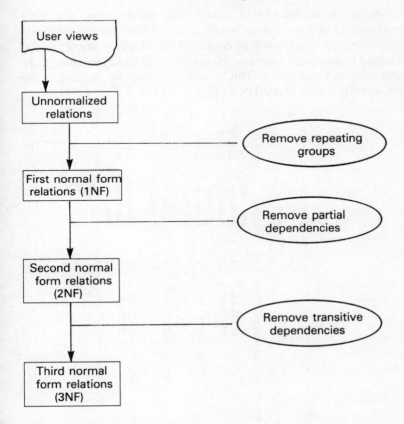

Fig. 3.10 The process of normalization

Universal relations

Sufficient information should have been obtained from the data-investigation stage to enable a relation to be created which contains attributes representing all of the real-world objects of interest; this is referred to as a universal relation, and is the first version of the model to be considered. Some applications need data to be represented in more than one universal relation. This relation needs to be examined to ascertain whether it is unnormalized or in one of the higher normal forms.

Unnormalized relations

Data may be viewed as a table. An unnormalized relation is one that contains one or more repeating groups. As a result, there are multiple values at the intersections of certain rows and columns. The main disadvantage of unnormalized relations is that they contain redundant data. Some information will be contained in multiple locations, so that it would be necessary to update the data in all of these locations, if the data were to be amended. This is well illustrated by the data in the unnormalized table Order-UN in Figure 3.11.

Order no.	Supplier no.	Supplier name	Supplier address	Order date	ISBN	Quantity ordered	Title	Price
678	7415	Blackwells	16 The Avenue, Oxford	4/12/89	0-82112-462-3	1	Organic chemistry	£ 9.00
					0-84131-460-7	4	Alchemy	£10.00
					0-69213-517-8	20	Expert systems	£16.99
679	7480	Oxford University Press	Crest House Oxford	4/12/89	0-93112-462-1	2	Computer science	£21.99
680	7480	Oxford University Press	Crest House Oxford	5/12/89	0-82112-462-3	3	Organic chemistry	£ 9.00
681	7499	Simon House	Simon House Cambridge	6/12/89	0-71143-526-6	2	Bibliography	£19.00
					0-63322-891-7	4	Management theory	£26.99

Fig. 3.11 Order – UN: an unnormalized relation

The top three rows of Figure 3.11 are logically a single row in the table, as they have the same identifier (i.e. a common order number). Similarly lines 6 and 7 constitute a single logical row.

There are, therefore, multiple values in each of two logical rows in the ISBN, Quantity ordered, Title and Price columns, or several values of these attributes are associated with the row identifier Order number.

The first normal form

The first stage of normalization, conversion to first normal form, is to remove any data aggregates, or, in the table, to ensure that all row/column intersections contain only one value by removing repeating groups to form separate tables. A relation is in first normal form if it contains no repeating groups. In the example (Figure 3.12), ISBN, Quantity ordered, Title and Price are removed to another table, Order − book − 1NF, whose identifier is a combination of Order number and ISBN. The remaining attributes from Order − UN form another table, Order − supplier − 1NF.

Note that one attribute, in this case Order number, must appear in both tables, as a device for linking the tables together.

(a) *Order − book − 1NF*

Order no.	ISBN	Quantity ordered	Title	Price
678	0-82112-462-3	1	Organic chemistry	£ 9.00
	0-84131-460-7	4	Alchemy	£10.00
	0-69213-517-8	20	Expert systems	£16.99
679	0-93112-462-1	2	Computer science	£21.99
680	0-82112-462-3	3	Organic chemistry	£ 9.00
681	0-71143-526-6	2	Bibliography	£19.00
	0-63322-891-7	4	Management theory	£26.99

(b) *Order − supplier − 1NF*

Order no.	Supplier no.	Supplier name	Supplier address	Order date
678	7415	Blackwells	16 The Avenue Oxford	1/12/89
679	7480	Oxford University Press	Crest House Oxford	4/12/89
680	7480	Oxford University Press	Crest House Oxford	5/12/89
681	7499	Simon House Press	Simon House Cambridge	6/12/89

Fig. 3.12 First normal form

The first normal form is not ideal. Three anomalies will be encountered:

- *Insertion anomaly.* Should it be necessary to insert data for a new book, say its ISBN, title and price, we cannot insert these data until this book has been ordered at least once, since no attribute in the identifier may have a null value. Thus, both Order number and ISBN must have a value.
- *Deletion anomaly.* Suppose that an order for a book is to be deleted. Deletion of an order will lead to deletion of all data concerning the book, such as title and price, and this information will therefore be lost.
- *Amendment anomaly.* If the title of a book needs to be amended, it will be necessary to search for all occurrences of the title of the book. Since a book may appear on several orders, updating is inefficient and is likely to lead to inconsistencies in the data.

Insert, delete and update tests may be conducted in order to identify relations or tables that are only in first normal form and that need to be normalized further.

Second normal form

To eliminate the anomalies of the first normal form, it is necessary to remove partial functional dependencies. A relation is in second normal form if it:

- is already in first normal form, and
- any partial functional dependencies have been removed

To convert a relation to second normal form, it is necessary to create two new relations, one with attributes that are fully dependent on the primary key or identifier, and the other with attributes that are dependent on only part of that key or identifier. These two relations are in second normal form.

In the example (Figure 3.13), Order−book−1NF is split into Book−3NF and Order−book−3NF. Thus, the attributes Title and Price are not in the identifier and are not determined by the whole of the identifier, because they are not determined by order number. The two new tables are in second normal form, but as will become evident, they are also already in third normal form, so have been labelled Book−3NF and Order−book−3NF.

Relations in 2NF may again be subjected to the insert, delete and update tests. The situation is improved, in that, for instance, the updating of data can be achieved by only one amendment. For example, if the price changes, then only one row of Book – 1NF has to be updated. However additional refinement is still required, since in inserting, updating or deleting other data in a relation in 2NF anomalies will arise. These are caused by the existence of *transitive dependencies*. Transitive dependencies occur when one non-key attribute (or attribute not in the identifier) is dependent on one or more other non-key attributes. In this example, this is demonstrated by analysis of Order – supplier – 1NF.

Here, Supplier number, which is not part of the identifier, determines Supplier name and Supplier address, so these can be split off from the table Order – supplier – 1NF.

Thus Order – 1NF is split again into two tables Order – 3NF and Supplier – 3NF.

(a) *Book – 3NF*

ISBN	Title	Price
0-82112-462-3	*Organic chemistry*	£ 9.00
0-84131-460-7	*Alchemy*	£10.00
0-69213-517-8	*Expert systems*	£16.99
0-93112-462-1	*Computer science*	£21.99
0-71143-526-6	*Bibliography*	£19.00
0-63322-891-7	*Management theory*	£26.99

(b) *Order – book – 3NF*

Order no.	ISBN	Quantity ordered
678	0-82112-462-3	1
678	0-84131-460-7	4
678	0-69213-517-8	20
679	0-93112-462-1	2
680	0-82112-462-3	3
681	0-71143-526-6	2
681	0-63322-891-7	4

(c) *Order – 3NF*

Order no.	Supplier no.	Order date
678	7415	1/12/89
679	7480	4/12/89
680	7480	5/12/89
681	7499	6/12/89

(d) *Supplier – 3NF*

Supplier no.	Supplier name	Supplier address
7415	Blackwells	16 The Avenue Oxford
7480	Oxford University Press	Crest House Oxford
7499	Simon House Press	Simon House Cambridge

Fig. 3.13 Second and third normal form

Third normal form

A relation is in third normal form when it:

● Is in second normal form, and
● Contains no transitive dependencies.

The attributes of the final third-normal-form tables are summarized below. The attributes in italics are the identifiers of the tables.

Order (*Order number*, Supplier number, Order date)
Book (*ISBN*, Title, Price)
Order—book (*Order number, ISBN*, Quantity ordered)
Supplier (*Supplier number*, Supplier name, Supplier address)

Other aspects of normalization

Relations in 3NF are sufficient for most practical database applications. They achieve the basic objectives of normalization, that is to reduce redundancy and produce a set of stable data structures. Relations beyond third normal form also exist.

The Boyce/Codd Normal Form (BCNF) is a slightly more powerful form than the third normal form. Normalized tables can be created directly by applying the principle of the Boyce/Codd Normal Form.

This principle requires that in a table or relation 'every determinant must be a candidate identifier'. In other words, an attribute must be a possible identifier. If it is not, new tables should be produced in which the non-identifying determinant becomes a possible identifier in a new table.

Fourth and fifth normal forms also exist. Normalization to fourth normal form is concerned with the elimination of multivalued dependencies. This arises when there are three attributes (e.g. A, B and C) in a relation, and for each value of A there is a well-defined set of values of B and a well-defined set of values of C. However, the set of values of B is independent of set C, and vice versa. A relation is in fourth normal form if it is in BCNF and contains no multivalued dependencies. Both fourth and fifth normal forms are topics for more advanced study, and so will not be discussed further here.

It should be remembered that normalization is only a guide in data analysis. The analyst's skill must also be applied, and sometimes an analyst will choose not to normalize data to third normal form. For example, consider the following Customer relation:

Customer (*Name*, Street, City, Postcode)

The primary key of this relation is Name. However, the relation is in

2NF because there is a transitive dependency. A Postcode uniquely identifies a City. Normalization theory would suggest that Customer be converted to the following two relations in 3NF:

Customer (*Name*, Street, Postcode)
Location (*Postcode*, City)

In practice, however, the designer would probably choose not to decompose Customer because the attributes Street, City and Postcode are almost always used together as a unit.

Normalization creates a data model that is independent of software, and can therefore be mapped onto any suitable package or language. The tables become the candidate file structures where each attribute is a field and each row a record. Within each file there will be an identifier, which will become the key field, and be used to identify a particular record.

One of the limitations of the normalization approach is its restricted semantics. There is no distinction made between entity set and relationship set, and no type and existence characteristics of the relationships are shown. Also, in the normalization approach entities are linked by means of attributes, whilst in the entity—relationship approach entities are linked directly. Hence some attributes exist in the normalization model, purely to maintain a link, which are not required in the top-down approach.

Entity—relationship modelling and normalization

Entity—relationship modelling is an intuitive top-down approach. Normalization is a structured, formal bottom-up approach.

They are most appropriately used in conjunction with one another. An initial analysis using entity—relationship modelling should be conducted in order to identify entities, attributes and relationships. This should be followed by the application of normalization to the attributes in the resulting entity and relationship sets as a check on the basic model.

These two data-modelling approaches represent only two of the many data-modelling approaches that have been proposed. They are both well established and widely used, and serve to introduce some of the basic concepts associated with data modelling.

Database design

Mapping the conceptual model to the database schema

The next stage in the database-design process involves the development of a data model that can be supported by a specific DBMS. Ideally this stage should be unnecessary. Database-management systems should operate directly in terms of the logical structure and hide the details of the physical organization from the user. This would both simplify the user's task, and also allow the DBMS much greater freedom to adapt the physical organization for optimum performance. However most DBMSs do not have this capability and this second design stage is necessary. There are a number of different types of DBMS, most of which can be broadly categorized into one of the following: relational, network, hierarchical, and more recently binary relationship.

The relational, network and hierarchical approaches are all entity-based. The hierarchical approach was the first to be developed in the 1960s. It evolved from the realization that many real-world structures were hierarchical in nature. However, not all real-world structures are hierarchical, and network and relational systems developed subsequently, in order to overcome the limitations of hierarchical systems. Hierarchical and network systems provide physical organizations which can represent the overlap between files directly as links or pointers. Relational systems instead provide a means of correlating files in the relational 'Join' operator.

A major factor in the user's satisfaction or lack thereof with a database system is its performance. The performance of a system depends on the efficiency of the data structures used to represent the data in the database, and how efficiently the system is able to operate on these data structures.

The relational model

Relations have already been encountered as a fundamental concept in the normalization process of the last section. The relational approach to data modelling was introduced by E. F. Codd in the late 1960s, and is based on the mathematical concepts of relations and sets. A relation may be described by its name and associated attributes. An example might be:

Catalogued−book (*ISBN*, Title, Author, Year)

The italicized attribute, *ISBN*, is the identifier or primary key of the relation. Figure 3.14 is an example of a set of occurrences of the Catalogued−book relation. The actual record occurrences in a relation are referred to as tuples, or n-tuples (where n is the number of attributes in a relation).

The relation then is like a table, and has rows and columns. Each row corresponds to a record, and each column to a field.

The rules for the relational approach derive from the underlying mathematical theory. The basic rules are:

ISBN	Title	Author	Year
0-82112-462-3	*Organic chemistry*	A.J.Brown	1989
0-84131-460-7	*Alchemy*	R.M.Major	1987
0-69213-517-8	*Expert systems*	S.Estelle	1988
0-93112-462-1	*Computer science*	S.Estelle	1989
0-71143-526-6	*Bibliography*	J.Johns	1981

Fig. 3.14 Catalogued–book relation occurrences

- A relation must contain one type of row or record. Each row must contain a fixed number of attributes, all of which are explicitly named. Different kinds of records are held in different relations.
- Within a relation, the attributes are distinct, and repeating groups are not allowed, i.e. each attribute must be represented by one value, and not a set of values.
- Each occurrence or record in a relation is unique, i.e. there are no duplicate records.
- The order of occurrences or rows within the relation or table is indeterminate. The occurrences may appear in any order.
- The attributes within any column take their views from a domain of possible attribute values.
- New relations can be produced on the basis of a match of attribute values from the same domain in two existing relations. This formation of new tables is the essence of relational processing.

Creating the relational model

If the normalization approach to data analysis has been adapted, the result is a relational data model. This avoids the need to map the conceptual data model onto the DBMS.

If a conceptual model has been developed using the top-down approach by entity – relationship modelling, it is necessary to map this model onto a relational data model. This involves three stages:

(a) Creating one relation for each entity-and-relationship set. This relation should contain the attributes associated with that entity-and-relationship set.

(b) Mapping the relationships, so that the relationships between entities can be represented in the relations. This can be achieved either by
- the *relationship-relation* approach, where one relation is created for each relationship with attributes consisting of the primary keys of the related entities

or by

- the *foreign-key* approach, where for each set of related entities, the primary key(s) are placed in one of the entities as foreign keys. The various kinds of relationships must be considered.
(c) Completing the relations, by adding identifiers or primary keys, where these do not already exist.

This relational model, as discussed in the section on normalization, contains much of the information in the original entity – relationship model, except data on the degree and existence characteristics of relationships.

Relational schema

The final stage of the database design is the DBMS-specific conceptual schema and associated external schema. The DBMS conceptual schema is a description of the DBMS data model written in the relevant data-description language (or DDL). Each DBMS has a different DDL. However, in all relational DDLs each relation or table is defined independently by specifying the name of the relations, followed by the attributes associated with the relation. For each attribute the type and size must be specified. Figure 3.15 shows part of a simple relational schema in Structured Query Language (SQL) DDL.

```
CREATE TABLE   CATALOGUED-BOOK
        (Isbn   CHAR(13) NONULL,
        Author   CHAR(20) VAR NONULL,
        Title   CHAR(40) VAR NONULL,
        Publisher   CHAR(20) VAR,
        Year   CHAR(4),
        Classmark   CHAR(10) NONULL )

CREATE TABLE   BOOK
        (Book#   CHAR(5) NONULL,
        Shelf   SMALLINT,
        Isbn   CHAR(13) )

CREATE TABLE   PERSON
        (Person#   CHAR(5) NONULL,
        Name   CHAR(20) VAR NONULL,
        Address   CHAR(40) VAR NONULL,
        Status   CHAR(5) )

CREATE TABLE   LOAN
        (Book#   CHAR(6) NONULL,
        Person#   CHAR(5) NONULL,
        Date-due-back   CHAR(6) NONULL )
```

Fig. 3.15 Part of the Library relational schema in SQL DDL

The network model

The network approach is based on explicit links or pointers between related entities. The best-known network model is the Codasyl model. Codasyl stands for Committee on Data Systems Languages. This committee and its sub-groups, notably the Data Base Task Group (DBTG), have been responsible for conceiving and evolving this model. Many implementations of the Codasyl proposals exist, the best known being DMS. Codasyl models have been particularly successful in providing fast access to related data in large database environments since the explicit links can provide fast access to related data. The network model does require a large number of links, which may take up more storage space than the data records themselves.

The central concept of the network model is the 'set' or 'coset'. The coset is the means by which two or more related record types representing entity or relationship sets may be linked together. Thus the coset is a means of representing a relationship. Diagrammatically cosets are represented by Bachman diagrams as demonstrated below:

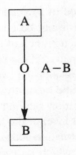

Here A and B are two record types and A−B is the relationship or coset. A is the owner-record type and B is the member. The relationship is implicitly one-to-many in the direction of the arrow. One-to-one relationships can be modelled in the same way, but many-to-many relationships have to be broken down into one-to-many relationships. A coset is represented in the database by a group of coset occurrences, each consisting of one owner record linked to a set of related records.

The members of a particular coset type may be classified as fixed, mandatory or optional. A record which is a *fixed* member must remain linked to the same owner throughout its life, a record which is a *mandatory* member must always be a member of that particular coset type but its owner within the coset may change, and finally a record which is an *optional* member may exist in the database without being linked into that particular coset type.

Using the coset, complex network structures can be built. A record type which is a member in one coset type may be a member of other coset types, and may also be an owner of other coset types.

Mapping from the conceptual model to the codasyl network

This involves the following stages:

(a)   The entity – relationship model is mapped into a Bachman diagram. This involves mapping entity-and-relationship sets into record types, and one-to-one and one-to-many relationships into cosets. Many-to-many relationships are broken down into one-to-many relationships. Cosets are labelled either F (fixed), M (mandatory) or O (optional).

(b)   Attributes are associated with record types.

(c)   The schema is represented in the codasyl DDL.

The hierarchical model

A hierarchy is a restricted form of network. It is a network in which the object can be connected to (owned by) only one object higher up in the hierarchy, although it can be connected to (own) many objects at a lower level. Thus at each branch of the hierarchy, there can be only a one-to-one or a one-to-many relationship with the next branch. The presence of a many-to-one relationship would create a network structure.

Figure 3.16 shows a simple hierarchical model. For each catalogued book there will be information relating to each copy of the book and each reservation at the first level of the hierarchy. For each copy of the book there will be loan information and also information about the person to whom the book is lent, which will include loan-status information. For each reservation there will be information about the person who has made the reservation, again including loan-status information.

The parent file can be searched through primary or secondary indexes. Each record in the parent file contains a pointer to a chain of records in the subordinate files. When a parent record is retrieved, the pointer can be used to retrieve all the subordinate records associated with it. This is faster than an index search.

This simple model illustrates the two fundamental problems with a hierarchical model:

● *Duplication.* Person information must be repeated in different occurrences of the hierarchy, since the same person may both borrow and reserve a book.

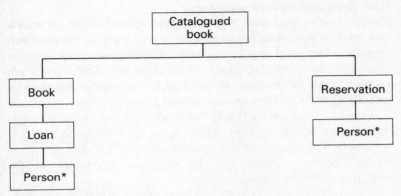

*includes loan-status data

Fig. 3.16   A single-hierarchy data model

- *Data access*. In a hierarchical model access to data is through the parent file, in this case 'catalogued book'. To find data on a particular person, for example, it is necessary to scan through the database, since there is no direct access by person.

A development of the hierarchy model is the multiple-hierarchy version, as shown in Figure 3.17. Some duplication remains, but data can be accessed directly from person, and data about individual persons can exist independently of whether they have reservations or not.

This may be taken further to a linked multiple hierarchy, which is essentially a limited network model. The best-known hierarchical system is IBM's IMS. This supports network structures by means of linked hierarchies.

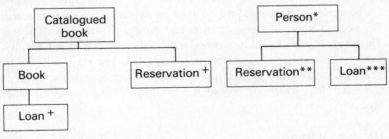

```
+      includes person identifier
*      includes loan-status data
**     includes ISBN
***    includes ISBN and book identifier
```

Fig. 3.17   A multiple-hierarchy model

User views and an external schema

The last few sections have been concerned with the construction of a conceptual schema which provides the overall view of the database. However, individual users may only be interested in, or may be constrained to, particular subsets of the databases. Such subsets are referred to as user views or external models, and may be described by an external schema. These external schemas must be consistent with the conceptual schema and the DBMS data model. The external schema may be described in various ways depending on the DBMS. An external-schema DDL similar to the conceptual-schema DDL may be provided, or the external schema may be expressed by means of the query/manipulation language statements.

User views are concerned with access to data. Access requirements may be recorded in terms of:

● The entities, attributes and relationships used
● The types of access required to support the various processes
● The access keys required
● The frequency of access
● The response times required.

These are issues which are explored in greater detail in Chapter Four, which focuses more directly on the design of the user interface.

Database implementation

Database implementation is part of the implementation of a complete computer system. The first step in database implementation involves reviewing the software available to establish the database. This should also have been considered at an earlier stage in the systems-analysis project, but options may be reviewed at this stage in order that a selection can be made and the second step in database implementation can proceed. The second step is the organization and storage of data in a database. This needs to be followed by a consideration of query processing. Finally, database protection needs to be organized. This last stage will not be discussed further here, since it involves aspects such as security, integrity and reliability, which are considered in Chapter Five, alongside other aspects of system security.

Database software

There is a wide variety of different software packages which support the creation of databases on microcomputers, minicomputers and mainframe computers.

Options that may be encountered by the information professional include:

(a) *Flat-file systems*, which are essentially electronic versions of a card index. More common in the microcomputer environment, these packages handle only one file at a time and are limited in the modifications that can be made to the database once it is defined and the number of fields in a record. All records are usually of the same length and fields are typically fixed length.

(b) *Database-management systems (DBMSs)* operate with several files or records at the same time, and support the creation of relational and other databases.

Typically, network and hierarchical DBMSs are most likely to be found on mainframe or minicomputers, since such systems generally provide good facilities for the management of large databases. On the other hand, most micro DBMSs are based on the relational model, but they vary in sophistication and user-friendliness. Another major distinction between mainframe systems and micro systems is in the language available for data manipulation. Mainframe systems tend to be hosted by a conventional general-purpose programming language (e.g. Cobol, Pascal); this is consistent with an environment in which applications are usually developed by experienced programmers. In the micro environment, on the other hand, the applications are usually relatively small and are written by non-specialists who will appreciate a self-contained and user-friendly language.

(c) *Text-retrieval packages* are designed specifically to handle a database of textual information. Typically, they have facilities for handling variable-length fields and sophisticated search facilities to support retrieval from textual databases. The emphasis is usually on one database, rather than drawing information from several databases, and the implementation often involves one specific application.

(d) *Custom-built packages*, designed and programmed specifically by a consultant or other systems designer for a specific application, often using an applications generator or data-description language such as is available in most database-management systems.

(e) *Library housekeeping systems* are purpose-built software packages, sometimes available as part of a hardware and software turnkey package, which support acquisitions, cataloguing, circulation control, management and online public-access catalogues. These packages create databases to support these various functions. The scope for database design for individual systems implementation is normally very limited, but, nevertheless, one of the approaches outlined in this chapter should underlie the design of databases in those systems.

The following checklist summarizes some features that might be sought in a good database-management system. Although not all software has all of these features, this list offers a set of criteria for the evaluation of database software packages.

Checklist of characteristics of a good database-management system

1 *General*
Single- and multi-user options, and appropriate security.
Works in the same way under a variety of operating systems including MS-DOS, OS-2, Xenix, Unix, etc.
New releases
Evaluation version
Many other users and user group

2 *Database structure*
Independence of data and program
No limits on: number of characters in a record
number of fields in a record
number of records in a database
Variable-length records and fields
New fields can be incorporated into existing databases
Screen editing and layout facilities
Validation procedures for data input
Control of privacy and integrity of data

3 *System design*
Easy systems design
User-defined screens, reports and menus, which can optionally be designed without programming, through a menu interface
Programming language for development of customized applications, with a built-in compiler
Programming possible with standard programming languages such as BASIC, C and Pascal
Royalty-free run-time version for applications operators

4 *Retrieval*
Query facilities of a high level

Fast retrieval based on inverted files of text words
Retrieval on any field in a record
Variety of search facilities including Boolean logic, searching on strings, hypertext

5 *Integration and interface*
Ability to move data to and from other database packages, e.g. dBase IV
Ability to integrate database data with word-processor, spreadsheet, graphics packages and their data

6 *Support*
Technical support and assistance
Training — in-house and on-site
Consultancy and configuration for specific applications
Database recovery and conversion

Database organization and storage

Once the conceptual model of the proposed system has been agreed, attention will turn to the design of the physical model, or the *internal model*. This involves two aspects, application design and file design. Application design is explored in Chapter Four. The issues that must be considered during file design are considered briefly here. Some aspects of file design are usually under the control of the user implementing a specific application, whereas others will be predetermined by the database software.

Application design and file design are closely interrelated. Application design is concerned with the human-computer interface, and the speed of access required at these interfaces is a major influence on file design.

The aim of file design is to convert the conceptual model into an efficient and workable physical structure. The physical structure may differ considerably from the conceptual structure. A number of conflicting factors must be taken into account in file design. These can be summarized as:

(a) *Operational purpose* of the file. What type of application is being considered? Will the file be accessed and updated online, or only accessed online?
(b) *Hardware* available for creating and storing the file. Both the hardware that is currently available and any possible improvements must be considered.
(c) *Software*. Again what database software is currently available?

Is it important in the interest of standardization to make use of existing software? Can the purchase of new software or an upgrade of existing software be justified?

(d) *File activity*, including how often the file is accessed and whether those accesses are enquiries or updates. For example, for update, the frequency with which files are updated, the number of amendments per update, the number of records on the file that need to be accessed on an update, and the length of time that updates take.

(e) *File volatility* and stability relates to the length of time that records stay in files. Indexed random files are better than indexed sequential files for volatile files.

(f) *Output requirements* may dictate the most appropriate file organization. A file may need to be processed in more than one way, and the chosen file organization must cater for different output and processing requirements.

(g) *Inputting requirements*. Files may be accessed by one transaction at a time, or transactions may be grouped and applied to the file in a single pass. The first of these is most common in online systems, although the second can be used to good effect in systems which do not require a response after every transaction.

(h) *Sorting requirements*. Large files are consuming to sort, and if a file is to be frequently sorted it may be preferable to split one large file into several smaller files. Another solution is to set up an index to the file with the index containing only the key of each record and the specific field or data item, or items required, and to sort the index.

(i) *Cost*. Some types of file organization may offer greater speed of access at the cost of extra storage space which will, in turn, increase hardware costs.

(j) *File access requirements*. These will be of two types: operational and informational. Operational access is required for routine processing. It is necessary to know the average volume over a particular timescale, and the presence, timing and size of any fluctuations, together with the response times required for each process. Informational access requirements are user enquiries on data stores. It is necessary to know the expected volume and frequency of each enquiry type, as well as their relative importance to the user.

There may be some conflicts between operational and informational access requirements which need to be solved. The designer needs to know:

- the keys on which the file will be accessed
- the necessary accesses between files
- the required speed of response.

Developing the physical database design
The physical design process should proceed in three stages:

- Development of initial physical design
- Evaluation of design
- Modification of physical design.

Through this process it is necessary to deal with record design and file design. Many aspects of the physical design are dependent upon the conceptual model. Factors to be considered include:

(a) *The record content* should follow from the conceptual model. Each normalized relation becomes a record type and each entity a field. The primary identifier becomes the record key.

(b) *Physical representation of data.* The various methods of storing data on magnetic storage media need to be reviewed.

(c) *The record size* must be decided in accordance with the length of data to be stored in records. Record lengths may be fixed or variable.

(d) *Records in a file.* The grouping of records into files needs to reflect the conceptual model. In the initial design one file is made for each record type, unless access would be more efficient if records of more than one type were stored together.

(e) *File organization.* Various options exist: direct, inverted, indexed sequential, serial and algorithmic. Choice will depend primarily on whether random access or sequential access is required, tempered by the file volatility.

(f) *File sequence.* The physical sequence of records in a file is chiefly determined by organization. For serial files, it is the sequence that records were written to file. For algorithmic files, it is determined by the algorithm. With direct file organization, the records can be in any order. In the case of an indexed sequential file the data are organized in the sequence of the primary key.

(g) *Record keys.* In a single-record file the record key will follow from the normalized data structure. However, in multiple-record files it will be necessary to construct appropriate record keys, which will consist of a key to the data structure or item, plus a record-type indicator.

  Some specifications may also require direct access to files on keys other than the main key. The need for those secondary keys should be carefully examined, and the number of secondary indexes kept to a minimum.

(h) *Physical file characteristics* such as the file's block size, overflow-area size and positioning on a physical device must finally be settled.

Once the physical design has been established, it must be tested and evaluated by matching it against the system requirements. Should amendments to the design prove necessary, there are four basic strategies that need to be investigated in any attempt to improve the design:

● Combination of records
● Splitting of records
● Amalgamation of records
● Alterations of processing mode.

It may be necessary to experiment with more than one of these strategies before a satisfactory physical design can be selected.

The final stage of database implementation is the input of data into the database. This is considered in Chapter Five.

Conclusion

This chapter has explored the various stages in database design, with an emphasis on data modelling, database design and database implementation. It has been impossible to explore all proposed strategies for these phases of database design, but key approaches and concepts have been introduced, from which readers may, if they choose, move on to a more advanced study of this topic. Clearly, an important adjunct to any reading about database design is experience with data modelling of real applications, and the use of database software packages.

Further reading

Avison, D. E., *Information systems development: a database approach*, Oxford, Blackwells, 1985.

Bowers, D. S., *From data to database*, Wokingham, Van Nostrand Reinhold (UK), 1988.

Dean, S. M., *Principles and practice of database systems*, Basingstoke, Macmillan, 1985.

Downs, J. E., *Basic systems design*, London, Hutchinson, 1985.

Frank, L., *Database theory and practice*, Wokingham, Addison-Wesley, 1988.

Hanson, O., *Design of computer data files*, London, Pitman, 1982.

Korth, H. F. and Silberschatz, A., *Database system concepts*, New York and London, McGraw-Hill, 1986.

Oxborrow, E., *Databases and database systems: concepts and issues*, Bromley, Chartwell-Bratt, 1986.

Sherman, G., *Introduction to databases on microcomputers*, Wokingham, Addison-Wesley, 1987.

Chapter Four

Human – computer interface design

Introduction

Chapter Three has considered data analysis and the progress from the conceptual model to the physical model of the database.

This chapter focuses on the human – computer interface, or what might otherwise be described as application design. Application design cannot be divorced from database design simply because the content of database must be determined by what users put into it, and what they want to get out of it. This might be termed the user schema as in Chapter Three, or the system access requirements. A number of the considerations relating to input and output design, especially the input- and output-item definitions, are crucial data which are central to the data-modelling process described in Chapter Three. They are however included in this chapter because they also form a basis for human – computer interface design. Application design and database design must proceed side-by-side, although for convenience they are examined separately in this text.

The human – computer interface can be defined in different ways, but the definition that is used here is that the user interface is those parts of the system with which the user comes into contact. This includes all input and output devices.

It is generally accepted that an interface should be *user-friendly*. User-friendliness is a relative concept, in that it must take into account the individual user. This has led to the adaption of user interfaces for different groups of users. A user-friendly interface is one that caters for different users equally effectively. The interface should present no barriers to the naive user who should be able to learn quickly and easily. For the experienced user, the interface must be able to support complicated functions and activities without cumbersome and irritatingly unnecessary support.

The interface should allow the inexperienced user to learn gradually how to deal with more complex problems. The best user interfaces should minimize the need for user training (which is discussed more fully in Chapter Five).

Interfaces involve output and input. Output or display of messages and results should provide maximum comprehensibility, whilst input should be associated with minimum effort and minimum opportunity for error. A good interface should:

- Offer *graceful interaction*, so that the user is notified when an error has been made, and the kind of error is identified immediately and in terms that the user understands.
- Be *compatible* with other interfaces that users have encountered and with their customary approach to a specific task.
- Be *consistent*.
- Be *flexible* with regard to minor errors.
- Inform the user of *delays*.
- Be *fail-safe*, so that any request for large change is verified before it is put into effect.
- Be *transparent*, so that the steps in, say, a retrieval process are hidden from the user, as far as is useful.

User-friendly interfaces are not merely a target for systems designers to strive towards. They should increase the effectiveness of the use of the system.

Users

Many attempts have been made to categorize types of computer-system users. Such users may be old or young, keen or apprehensive, clever or dim, determined or lazy, willing or reluctant, and so it goes on. There is an endless supply of research topics in trying to identify those characteristics of users that affect the way in which they interact with a computer system. There are only two indisputable facts. The first is that the quality of the human — computer interface and the user's experience of the system will influence the quality and accuracy of the data that are input to the system and the appropriateness of the data that are extracted and used from the system. The second is that the human — computer interface must be tailored to the requirements, perspectives and activities of the users for whom it is intended.

A user's facility with any given computer system depends initially upon:

- His previous experience with that system (if any)
- His previous experience of similar systems that perform the same function (e.g. other word-processing software)

- His familiarity with the functions required in the tasks that the system is designed to perform (possibly gained through working with a manual system that performs similar tasks)
- His previous experience of computer systems in general
- His ability and willingness to learn
- His attitude to change
- How well the user dialogues that he encounters in the system are tailored to his requirements.

It is helpful to view users as falling into three main categories:

- Casual and novice users, who have little or no knowledge of what is expected of them
- Experienced users who will need little prompting information to guide them in the system's use
- Computer-professional users, who may require additional power and flexibility in their interface with the system.

It should, however, be remembered that the lines between these categories are blurred. For example, we may add to this list:

- Occasional users, who did know what was expected of them, but have forgotten.

Also novice users can become experienced users, and experienced users may eventually need the same flexibility as computer-professional users.

 Novice users in general have no prior knowledge of what is expected of them and no preconceptions of what the computer system is going to do. They need to be guided step-by-step through their interaction with the system. Any dialogue must use terms with which the user is familiar. Experienced users need little information to guide them in system use. Indeed too many prompts may slow down the interaction with the system and irritate the user. However, experienced users have a variety of different levels of experience and are likely to be more familiar with some parts of the system than others. Guidance must be available when the experienced user requires it, possibly by changing the character of the prompts or through calling upon a help system. Computer-professional users need the same kind of guidance as experienced users, but may demand more power, speed and flexibility in their interaction with the computer.

Another categorization which is worth making is the division into types of users according to their status in relation to the system. These may include:

- Staff responsible for the computer system

- Staff responsible for the data and services associated with the computer system, e.g. records, managers and information officers
- Staff of the organization who are users of the system
- Users, such as the general public and students.

These categories of users will require different kinds of dialogues, not only because they may have different levels of familiarity with the system, but also because they may be permitted and will choose to perform different functions in relation to the system.

In addition to these factors which may be relatively easy to identify, aspects of the users' wider environment may also influence their response to the system. These may include aspects such as the extent of interruption, expectations of the system, extent of time pressure and urgency. Obviously other factors which are well beyond the system designer's control, such as family, health, economic and social issues, can also influence individuals as system users. Although there may be little that the system designer can do to control these factors, he may be able to alleviate the effects of such factors on data quality etc. by sound validation routines and security measures.

Input and output procedures

Input procedures are the procedures through which all data and programs are entered into the computer. Output procedures are the means by which data and programs are made available from the computer after processing. Since input and output devices and procedures represent the main contact that users have with computer systems, it is important that they be designed so that they give the user a positive view of the system.

In assessing input and output devices a number of general features that are important for any hardware must be considered. They are:

- Delivery time
- Simplicity of installation
- Reliability
- Maintenance support
- Compatibility
- Supplier stability and credibility.

In addition, human-aspects criteria must be considered. Important here are:

- Workplace characteristics of the equipment should match the physical requirements of the human user.
- Equipment controls and operating activities must be logical, consistent and easy to understand.

- Equipment display features and screen formats must be logical, consistent and easy to understand.
- Environmental factors may place special constraints on equipment choice, such as outdoor use, portable use.
- Documentation to aid installation, maintenance, etc.
- Training and support from the manufacturers to assist in system installation, implementation and modification.

The input and output requirements of the system will have already been defined in outline in the conceptual model of the system. The design process develops this model, checks the practicability and desirability of input and output, and determines the media and processes for capturing input data and generating output.

The logical model of the system is specified in the logical specification in terms of dataflow diagrams (DFDs), data dictionaries (DDs) and other data-analysis techniques. Inputs and outputs should be readily identifiable by examining the boundaries of the DFDs. The process which is just inside the boundary of the DFD is the human–computer interface.

Input design

The collection of data is often the most expensive part of the system, and certainly represents a significant proportion of the continuing costs of a system. Data input is also the stage during which most errors enter the system, so careful attention must be paid to the minimization of errors during input. The objectives of input design are to:

- Choose a cost-effective method of input
- Choose an appropriate method of input for the application and user
- Design procedures for minimizing errors.

This process involves a number of stages:

- Defining the data to be input
- Considering input media
- Examining and selecting input processes
- Designing error minimization techniques
- Documentation.

Input-item specification

The input-item specification indicates the nature of each type of input item. Documents designed for data input should be specified formally as part of the installation documentation. Typically it is useful to record, for each item:

- Identification, such as a code, for recognition as a kind of data item
- Content and format of the data item, including the content of every field, the meaning of any control symbols, the relationship between fields and control symbols, and the inter-relationships between fields
- Frequency of receipt
- Expected volumes of data
- Conditions or factors which cause the appearance of a new data item in the system
- Sequence in which the items will be received for processing
- Any validation procedures to be employed to ensure accuracy
- Statement of any pre-sorting and batching for control purposes
- Statement of any manual editing etc. prior to data input
- Source of the document, e.g. the department that generates the data.

The National Computing Centre provides a useful prompt sheet to cover input-item specification.

Input devices

A review of the variety of input devices is given below:

- Punched input, including cards, tags and paper tape
- Magnetic input such as is generated on tape or disc by key-to-magnetic tape, key-to-disc, key-to-diskette and key-to-cassette units
- Magnetic ink character recognition (MICR)
- Optical character recognition (OCR)
- Optical marks
- Light pens and bar codes
- Computer input and microfilm
- Speech
- Handwriting
- Other media such as graphics tablets, touch-sensitive screens, joysticks and trackerballs, mice, magnetic cards, facsimile-transmission devices, sensors and computer vision
- VDU terminals and their associated keyboards. Function keys may be used to aid rapid data entry.

These methods can be broadly categorized:

- Those that convert data into a computer-readable medium by people using a keyboard
- Those that read data directly into a machine-readable format, e.g. OCR, OMR and MICR

- Those that involve exchange of data between or downloading from computer systems.

The choice of input method must depend on the application. Some of the factors that determine the most apt input method are:

(a) *Type of processing.* Items may appear for processing in batches or groups of records, or individually. Batches may be sorted or unsorted (random).

(b) *Speed of data preparation and capture.* For example, OCR involves no data preparation (provided that the data are in the correct format), but OCR devices read data into the computer relatively slowly.

(c) *Accuracy and verification.* Some methods of data input are inherently more accurate than others, and some facilitate ready verification of data. One general point is that the fewer times data are transcribed or handled, the less chance there is that inaccuracies will creep in. Various methods of verification are possible, including sight, re-entry and parity checking.

(d) *Cost* must be considered both in terms of the capital cost of equipment, and also in terms of the cost per character or cost per item of input. This second category of cost will involve staff costs, and possibly telecommunication costs. Costs of floor-space, supplies, back-up facilities and re-design of the working environment may all need to be considered.

(e) *Suitability for application.* Some of the more specialist forms of data-input device have been designed to meet the requirements of a particular application. For example, Kimball tags hang well on clothes, bar codes are easy to stick on many items including books.

(f) *Rejection rate*, or the percentage of items of input which will not be acceptable to the system. What is the error rate and how will errors be handled? Routines for data correction must be considered.

(g) *Operator requirements* cover what is required of the operator, such as wanding or keying, and how compatible these operations are with the operator's wider environment. In addition, training requirements of operators must be considered, especially if there are large numbers of operators, and staff turnover is high.

   Also any requirements for instructions or documentation must be considered.

(h) *Security.* Aspects such as loss of input forms, corruption of data (especially data already in the database), fraud and other damage to the data need to be considered.

(i) *Volume* of data to be processed.

(j) *Overall system timing.*

Input processing

Inputting of data is usually labour-intensive if large quantities of data are to be handled. The input process involves some or all of:

- Data recording at source
- Data transcription into an input form
- Data conversion to a computer-readable medium
- Data control, including checking batching and controlling dataflow to the computer
- Data transmission to computer
- Data validation and verification
- Error correction
- Control over movement and processing of data.

Ideally, data should be recorded in machine-readable form as a by-product or integral part of the actual transmission, and the data should be recorded as the transaction occurs. This eliminates the first two stages above and is therefore more efficient, but it can be done only with appropriately located terminals and trained staff.

Each input method has inherent characteristics in respect of these features. These inherent characteristics must be matched with user requirements in the selection of the optimum input method.

The design of input processes should be completed with a consideration of error avoidance and input documentation. Error avoidance is considered in more detail in Chapter Six where security is considered. Input documentation is considered at the end of this chapter together with all kinds of user documentation.

Output design

Output is what emerges from a computer system for the user to act upon. A system may, with justification, be judged by the quality of its output. Output may take one of several forms including:

- Reports of data from the system to staff
- Documents for communication with customers or clients
- Hard copy for later reference
- Hard copy for back-ups
- Data to be re-input to this system or to another system.

Outputs may be internal or external. External outputs, to people outside the organization, need careful design since they convey an image of the organization. Both internal and external outputs may be either interactive (on screen) or hard copy.

In addition to these items, which could be described as 'proper' output, there will also be output in the form of messages and instructions that relate to operating the system itself. This is of two kinds:

- Prompts, which indicate to the user that some input is required, and more helpfully what kind of information is required
- Instructions and messages about the system, such as help messages and error messages.

There are four main methods of output:

- Printing to produce hard copy
- Screen display
- Microfilm, especially for archival copies and other bulky items, such as catalogues
- Synthetic speech, which is still limited in application.

The first of these two are the most common.
    There are many kinds of printers. Some options are:

- Line printers
- Daisywheel printers
- Dot-matrix printers
- Ink-jet and ink-dot printers
- Thermal, electrostatic and electrosensitive printers
- Thermal-transfer printers
- Laser printers
- Graphic printers.

Each of these offers different opportunities for the quality and design of printed output. The wider availability of cheaper good-quality laser printers over the last two years has made a significant impact on the quality of output available and there are also good quality dot-matrix printers.

Output-item definition
Before embarking on any plans for output it is important to establish that the output is necessary, and that the cost of output can be justified. Each data item should be identified in the dataflow diagrams in the requirements specification.
    It may also be necessary to analyse the required form of the data output since the data may not be held in the database in exactly the form in which they are to be output. This can be achieved by the development of an output-item definition. Such a definition should evolve from consultation between the user and the analyst.
    The output-item definition should cover:

- Type of output
- Content of output, including fields, and any summary statistics and a written description of the data contents of the form
- Format and layout of output, including the order of any discrete items, headings, sub-headings, some representative data items and any totals (see section below on forms design)
- Location of output (especially with screen-based output, where output may not be available at all required locations)
- Frequency of output, e.g. monthly, daily, on-demand
- Response time, e.g. on-demand output, or processing required prior to output
- Any volume statistics concerning output that are required
- Post-printing requirements, such as folding, stapling and envelope stuffing
- How users can exercise control over output, especially in interactive systems.

It is important to record the decisions taken for later reference. Various of the National Computing Centre forms can assist with this process. The NCC Record-Specification form can be used to record the data contents of the output, as each item can be regarded as a computer-record type. The NCC Computer-Document-Specification Form assists in recording aspects of the document, such as its title, number of parts, lines per page, numbered pages, stationery reference etc. and the NCC Display Chart helps in design of the layout of information.

Choice of output method

There is normally a choice between screen-based output and a number of different printer-generated outputs. The factors that may be debated in choosing output method include:

- Response time demanded
- Quality of output required
- Number of 'copies' required
- Volumes of output
- Whether a hard-copy record is desirable for convenience or security
- What peripherals exist or can be obtained
- Whether the system is integrated or not
- Effective cost
- Compatibility of the output equipment with the remainder of the computer system
- Extent of user control over output — can users choose different outputs on different occasions?

- Whether on-demand or automatic output is available
- Location of users, and recipients of the output
- Software and hardware availability.

Output processing

Output processes depend on the type of output. Screen design, forms and dialogue design are discussed specifically later. Output control is important. Security aspects of output control are tackled in the section on security in Chapter Six.

Interface and dialogue design

The dialogue between the user and computer in an online system is an important part of the human−computer interface. It is instructive to view the dialogue as a conversation between the user and the computer. The primary objective of the dialogue is that both participants understand each other. As we have already noted, users come to a computer system with different levels of experience and with differing attitudes. Dialogues must cater for all expected users equally well, and as a first step in dialogue design it is important to collect information concerning:

- User activities which will determine the required dialogues and their objectives
- Dialogue users, their backgrounds, previous system experience and frequency of use of the system which will be necessary in determining the dialogue style
- Jargon, abbreviations and codes which are understood by the user
- Equipment and software and any constraints that these impose
- Any existing dialogue design standards that have already been established in the organization. If no such standards exist then any dialogues should be made as compatible as possible with the dialogues the users currently experience.

Having gathered this preliminary information, some general advice needs to be heeded before embarking on dialogue design. Points to be remembered include:

- Dialogue design takes time and effort, especially if a large number of dialogues are to be designed to cover a variety of different activities
- Dialogue design standards should be established and used
- Design a flexible dialogue, that can be amended to accommodate changes in activities and users. User activities will change, experienced users will move and be replaced by new users, and novice

users will become experienced users
- The dialogue should be logical, and related points should be grouped together. Consultation with the user during the design process will facilitate the logical structuring of the dialogue.

Dialogue design stages

Dialogue design can seem a daunting task. It is useful to break the process into more manageable stages. Each of these stages will be necessary for each dialogue in a system, although most of the decisions will be made for the first dialogues to be designed and carried over to later dialogues which should adhere to similar styles and standards. It is assumed that a preliminary step is to establish the purpose of the dialogue and the potential users.

The stages then are:

(a) Identification of the data elements which are likely to occur in the course of the dialogue. These might, for example, include names, codes, indexing terms and commands.

(b) Establishment of response times and any terminal requirements, then selection of dialogue styles. Dialogue styles are discussed more fully below.

(c) Analysis of the dialogue into discrete blocks on related issues and identification of the objectives of each block. The order of the blocks should be determined.

(d) Dialogue design for each block, taking into account both the range of user responses and the computer's response to each of these.

(e) Design of validation procedures and error messages.

(f) Integration of the dialogue with the system including formatting the screen. The first five stages are concerned with the data to be exchanged; this stage moves on to consider how the dialogue should be displayed on the screen, and other terminal requirements. Terminal requirements include terminal memory capacity, function keys etc. Formatting of screens can be made easier with screen pointers and application-program generators, such as are available as an integral part of much database software.

(g) Testing and modification, in consultation with users. Testing must be to exhaustion covering all possible user and machine responses.

(h) Implementation.

Dialogue styles

There are a number of different dialogue design styles (see Figure 4.1).

		Advantages	Disadvantages
1	*Menus*	Easy to learn. Easy to use. Easy to program. Suitable for novice users in access to system options.	Slow to use in large systems. Limited choice per menu. Transmission overhead. Can be irritating to experienced users.
2	Icons	Very easy to learn. Easy to use. Language independent. Relatively easy to program. Suitable for novice users in system access and command interfaces.	Not economic in use of screen space. Needs some text back-up. Requires graphics hardware. Needs icon-builder software.
3	*Question and answer*	Easy to use. Easy to learn. Easy to program.	Unsophisticated. Slow to use.
4	*Form filling*	Quick to use. Easy to use. Easy to learn. Suitable for all user types, data entry, display and retrieval interfaces.	Form only suitable for data entry. Unsophisticated.
5	*Command languages*	Quick to use. Sophisticated. Extensible. Suitable for expert users with complicated requirements.	Difficult to learn. Difficult to use for novices. Difficult to program.
6	*Natural language*	Natural communication. No learning required. Suitable for novice users in a restricted problem domain.	Difficult to program. Needs knowledge base. Verbose input. Can be ambiguous.

Fig. 4.1 Dialogue-design styles

Areas where group into relevant areas this auto the use as it is more logic

A number of these may be used at different places in the same interface, to meet the tasks to be completed by the user. Furthermore, the categories are not exclusive or independent. Voice systems will eventually become a form of natural-language interface and icons are a different way of presenting menus.

1 *Menu selection* dialogues involve presenting the user with a number of alternatives or a menu on the screen, and asking him to select one of them if he wishes to proceed. The alternatives are usually displayed either as commands (for more experienced users) or as short explanatory pieces of text. Pictures or icons may also be used to represent the alternatives in the menu. One option is selected by keying in a code (often a number or letter) for that option, or by pointing to that option with a mouse or other pointing device. Menus are generally recognized to be a sound approach for the occasional or novice user. Additional help is rarely necessary, and little data entry is required of the user. Also, since any input must be one of the options offered, menu-based systems are straightforward to program.

The limitations of menus are:

● They are not suitable for inputting data such as numbers or text
● A lot of information is presented on the screen — this takes time to appear and time to read
● Only a limited number of options may be presented on one screen. In order to offer a large number of options it is necessary to design a hierarchy of menus
● Once a hierarchy of menus and sub-menus is included, it is important to give the user the means to keep track of where they are, and to be able to trace a path through the hierarchy.

A disadvantage of early menu-based systems was that significant parts of the screen were occupied by menus, leaving little space for work area. If menu choices are required at several points in a dialogue the need to replace a work area with a menu can be disruptive. Pop-up or pull-down menus overcome this problem, by being on display only when in use, and over-laying only a small part of the work area.

Guidelines for menu design

1 Group logically related options together either as menu blocks or in separate menu screens.
2 Order menu options by the usual criteria, such as operational sequence, frequency of use, importance etc.
3 Indicate the reply expected and associate it with the option.

4 Title the menu according to its function.
5 Give the user feedback about menu levels, errors etc.
6 Provide escape routes and bypasses, so that users can pass from one option to another without going up and down the hierarchy.

Menu interfaces have become a standard feature of database and library-housekeeping software over the past few years.

2 *Function keys* are a hardware equivalent of menus with options allocated to special keys on the keyboard. Function keys might cover options such as copy, insert, delete, help, display record, call menu.

Hard-coded function keys have an operation permanently allocated to a particular key, and are located accordingly. With soft-coded keys the command call is allocated to the function key by the application program. Most keyboards have 10−12 function keys, so the options that can be covered by these keys are limited.

3 *Icons* were pioneered by Xerox in the Star system, and by Apple in the Lisa and Macintosh interfaces. Icons are pictorial representations of objects in the system. Operation of the system is by selecting objects and moving them with the cursor. For example, to delete a file you move a folder into the waste-paper bin. Icons are realistic and their meaning can easily be deciphered.

Icons do however have limitations. These are:

● It is difficult to represent functional operations or abstract concepts such as 'check spelling' or 'global find and replace'.

● Ambiguity, for example the waste paper basket may be mistaken for a message bucket.

For these reasons the use of icons cannot be universal, but they do have a role in creating some very-easy-to-learn interfaces.

Guidelines on icon design
1 Test the icons with users.
2 Make icons as realistic as possible.
3 Give the icon a clear outline to help visual discrimination.
4 When showing commands give a concrete representation of the object to be operated upon.

4 *Direct manipulation* refers to interfaces which include icons, pointing and features associated with WIMP (Windows, Icons, Pop-up Menu) interfaces. In such interfaces the user sees and directly manipulates representations of objects in the system. Objects are shown as icons which can be addressed by pointing at them with a mouse or another similar cursor-control device. Pointing allows objects to be selected. Direct

manipulation allows objects to be moved around the screen in a dragging operation. In this way new associations between objects can be formed, as in, for example, a file being placed in a folder, and operations can be performed on objects. The interface supports the user's tasks by portraying a realistic 'virtual world' on the screen. Operation is supposed to be immediately obvious, and error messages are unnecessary. It can be difficult to represent the 'virtual world' with concrete icons, but nevertheless direct manipulation creates usable and appealing user interfaces.

5   *Windows* subdivide the screen space so that different operations can be taking place on the screen at the same time. There are two types of windows: *tiled*, where the screen is divided up in a regular manner into sub-screens with no overlap; and *overlapping*, where windows can be nested on top of each other, with either complete or partial overlapping.

Windows have a number of uses. Screen areas can be separated for error messages, control menus, working area and help. Two or more processes can be run in different windows, or two files can be pictured simultaneously. There is evidence that people work on more than one task at a time and the window environment supports multi-task processing. Use of windows is still relatively new, but it is clear that too many windows can be confusing as the screen becomes cluttered. Mistakes can be made as attention is distracted by something happening in a window not being worked on.

6   *Question and answer.* The user of a question-and-answer dialogue is guided through his interaction by questions or prompts on the screen. He responds to these by entering data through the keyboard. Often questions may require only a simple 'yes' or 'no' response, but on other occasions the user may be required to supply some data, such as a code, a password, his name or other textual data. Usually, however, one-word responses are expected. On receiving the user's response, the computer will evaluate it and act accordingly. This may involve the display of data, additional questions or the execution of a task such as saving a file. The prompt information can easily be tailored to the requirements of the user, and this dialogue style may therefore suit novice and casual users. The main drawback of this dialogue mode is that since an input data item must be validated at each step before continuing with the dialogue, the interaction can be slow.

7   *Form filling.* In a form-filling dialogue the user works with a screen-based image of a form. Form design is considered more fully later in this chapter. The screen form will have labels, and space into which data are to be entered. It should be possible to move a cursor to any appropriate

position on the form for the entering of data. Labels will normally be protected from amendment or overwriting and some users may be able to amend only certain fields, so that others are protected. Form filling is a useful dialogue mode for inputting records and blocks of data, and supports clerical keying of data into a database well. The screen form may be a duplicate of a paper form from which data are transcribed. All data input should be validated and errors reported to the user.

8 *Command languages.* In dialogues based on commands, the user enters his instructions as pre-set commands. The computer recognizes these commands and takes appropriate action. The command language for a given system is a feature of the software. There are command languages for operating systems (more evident to the user in microcomputer systems) and command languages for applications software. The user of the international online information services will be familiar with the various command languages used by the online hosts. The command language must include commands for all of the functions that the user might choose to perform, and therefore, since different systems perform different functions, it is inevitable that command languages will differ between systems. Some attempts have been made to adopt standard command languages for systems that perform similar functions, and one result of this is the Common Command Language used by some of the online hosts. However, standardization is difficult and an inherent feature of command-based dialogues is the need for users to be familiar with the command language used. An intermediate option which is suitable for users with some familiarity with the system is the use of menus with commands, so that users are prompted in their use of commands. This is not, however, effective for new users because they cannot be expected to know what the commands displayed on the menus mean.

Command languages are potentially the most powerful interface, but this brings the penalty of difficulty of learning. The main advantages of command languages are the economy of screen space, the direct addressing of objects and functions by name, and the flexibility of system function which a combination of commands can provide.

All command languages have a word set, described as a *lexicon*, and rules that state how words may be combined, which is a *grammar*.

The lexicon needs words to identify objects and operations. Objects will be devices, files, etc. which the commands of the language operate on. Objects will be described by nouns and operations by verbs. Both word sets need to be as meaningful as possible. Usually commands will be truncated. The norm is three-letter truncations, e.g.

DIR for DIRECTORY
DIS for DISPLAY

Care needs to be exercised to ensure that each abbreviation is unique, e.g.

DIS for DISPLAY
DIS for DISCONNECT

cannot co-exist in one command language.

The language syntax may be in the form of simple one-word keywords, or keywords where a qualifying argument or condition is added. The most sophisticated languages are grammar-based. Here a set of rules is introduced to formulate a set of phrases which may be divided by combinations of command words. The rules dictate which word types may occur in sequence within a command-word string. Some grammatical command languages have the complexity of programming languages. These are powerful and flexible, but impose a considerable learning burden on the user.

Design of command languages – some pointers
1 Command-word codes should be consistent.
2 Punctuation and use of delimiters should be minimized.
3 Entry should be flexible and forgiving. Double spaces between words should be ignored and mis-spellings corrected if possible.
4 Command words and syntactic sequences should be natural and familiar, e.g. COPY from file A to file B.
5 Limit unnecessary complexity.
6 Allow editing of the command string.

9 *Other screen-based dialogues*. The dialogue styles so far considered use letters and numbers. Natural-language and keyboard dialogues also use letters and numbers. In natural-language dialogues, for example, an attempt is made to give the impression that it is possible to talk to the computer in everyday language. However, computer systems have difficulty in coping with the inconsistency, ambiguity and confused syntax of most natural languages.

Expert and intelligent interfaces are an area to which much development effort is currently being devoted. These interfaces do not require the user to define precisely the information needed or to be able to express the query in terms appropriate to a retrieval system. These interfaces undertake some of these tasks for the user.

10 *Voice-based dialogues*. All the dialogues discussed so far are concerned with screen-based communication, with the aid of keyboards, mice, touch screens or similar devices. There are many circumstances

in which a voice-based dialogue would be most convenient for the user. Such dialogues would be attractive to the occasional user inputting only 'yes' and 'no' and other one-word answers and also to the user inputting large quantities of textual data. Voice-based dialogues might be voice-to-voice (i.e. computer and person talk to each other), screen-to-voice (i.e. computer displays data on screen, and person talks), or voice-to-keyboard (i.e. computer talks, person operates keyboard).

With voice-to-voice dialogues communication may be remote from a full terminal, through a telephone receiver and telecommunications link. All of these modes may have their applications, and the dialogue modes outlined above (e.g. menu, command, form filling) might be employed in a voice-based dialogue. Apart from experimental systems, such dialogues are still in the future, but they do need to be considered.

Colour in dialogue design

Many computer systems today have colour monitors, and software may use colour in screen displays. Using colour, especially in creating your own screen forms and dialogues, is fun but colour needs to be used with caution.

Some software packages just allow you to change the colour of the background and the text on the screen. Others use a variety of different colours in status bars, menus, main text etc. and permit changes to be made to any of these. Colour can be used to:

- Improve legibility and lessen eyestrain
- Highlight different parts of the screen display, e.g. status bars, menus
- Group elements in menus or status bars together, e.g. an instruction with the number for its function key.

Colour should be used with discretion. A screen that is appropriate for attracting attention at an exhibition is probably not appropriate for day-to-day working.

Some colour combinations are illegible or nauseous or otherwise objectionable. Colour does offer considerable scope for design, but also requires the application of some design talents. When designing screen interfaces that use colour, it is sometimes important that the interfaces be also capable of display on a monochrome monitor. The screen designer still needs to rely upon layout and lines for clarity.

Colour has three qualities:

- Wavelength, which determines the basic colour
- Saturation, or the amount of white mixed with a colour

● Brightness, or hue, the measure of colour luminance.

There is little information on the effects of these qualities and their interaction. However, general guidelines are:

● Limit the number of colours in one display to a maximum of five or six (although some prefer three or four)
● Display unhighlighted information in low saturation, low hue, or pale colours
● To show status: red = danger/stop; green = normal/proceed; yellow = caution
● To draw attention: white, yellow and red are the most effective
● To order data, follow the spectrum
● To separate data, choose colours from different parts of the spectrum
● To group data, choose colours which are close neighbours in the spectrum.

It is also important to note that colours have different qualities of subjective brightness and that colour affects shape resolution.

Graphics in dialogue design
Graphical displays in the design of human—computer interfaces are a relatively new innovation and an area in which there are continuing developments. The quality of the graphic display depends upon:

● The kind of monitor
● The range of colours available
● The use of graphics in software packages.

Graphics are in general used for impact, or to attract attention. They are common for title screens of software packages and have a role in help systems.

One specific area in which graphical displays are relatively well established is in the display of statistical data. A number of packages that are designed for handling this kind of data include facilities for producing: histograms, pie charts, line graphs and scatter diagrams. Some packages also offer options for three-dimensional displays in the form of three-dimensional histograms, multi-variate pie charts and three-dimensional line graphs. Hierarchy diagrams, network diagrams and finally, the use of symbols and icons can also contribute to an effective display. Some exciting options have been explored in the Hypercard retrieval system developed for the Apple Macintosh. In this system the user points (using a mouse or a pointing device) to a feature in a picture, which results in another more detailed picture; thus pointing to a hand on the picture of a body can produce a picture of a hand for closer examination.

Ten tips for dialogue design

1 Keep information displays brief.
2 Keep operator responses as short as possible, e.g. Y or N, not YES or NO.
3 Accept user responses in capitals or lower case unless it is really necessary to distinguish between them.
4 Respond to every entry, so that the operator is not left in suspense. Use messages, such as 'Please wait' or 'Sorting' if necessary.
5 Use clear formats with ample space.
6 Avoid difficult and unfamiliar jargon.
7 Make error correction easy.
8 Give clear error messages, showing as far as possible what the error is.
9 Provide a good 'Help' facility. The best 'Help' facilities explain the dialogue at the point of difficulty, show the effect of a command and explain how to continue.
10 Use default options as appropriate. Default options are the options that the user is most likely to want. Appropriate use of default options gives the user the opportunity to use the default option, or select others as needed.

Some dialogue-design gremlins

Good advice on dialogue design sounds like common sense. A recent catalogue of some dialogue-design faults in existing systems may serve to highlight some common errors to avoid. You can have some fun spotting these faults in software that you encounter.

● Large convoluted menu structures, in which even the menu-designer can get lost.
● Complicated command combinations that are difficult to learn.
● Entries that need complete re-typing if you get even one character wrong.
● Editing facilities, where it is possible to view, but not edit frames other than the one currently being edited; however, you cannot return to the one being edited after viewing another.
● Inconsistencies in:
   − methods of returning to earlier states
   − use of mouse buttons
   − structuring of menus

- terminology
- commands
- Names — in one system the whole software had the same name as part of the software.
- The order in which objects and the actions performed on them are selected can be illogical. Often systems require selection of action, then object, e.g. select 'update', then select database. Users are accustomed to holding the information and then deciding what to do with it.
- Ambiguities and sloppiness in instructions are common. A good example is 'Hit any key to continue' — this does not usually mean this as the SHIFT, CTRL and BREAK keys are not usually suitable, in that they will have a different (and often unpredictable) effect.
- Poor menu organization and use. Long menus with as many as 20 options have been encountered. These are acceptable only if the options are in a logical order and clearly structured. Overlapping options and ambiguous option labels are too common. Selection of menu option by entering a digit and then pressing return, or worse moving a cursor and then pressing return, is slow. Choice should be by a simple key press.
- The task-action mapping of systems is not always appropriate. In one system it was necessary to enter some of the new country data, then some of the new currency data, and then go back and complete both of these in turn.

Forms and screen design

The nature and purpose of forms

Forms abound in computer systems. They are a means of structuring information. They are particularly appropriate when the application is suitable for a database which will contain a number of records each of which holds similar data, but for a different person or item.

Forms may be printed or on screen, and may be used in input or output of data from a computer system. The specific characteristics of these various types of forms will be considered in detail later. All forms should be regarded as a means of communication and should be designed accordingly. A form is a means of:

- Obtaining or gathering information
- Disseminating information and sometimes storing information.

Form design can be performed by system users, especially where microcomputer systems are concerned. In such systems the database software will normally offer facilities for form design. However, the design of good-quality forms is a specialized skill, and where forms that are to be used by a large number of people are concerned, some centralization of form production is useful.

Many computer systems have a large number of forms associated with them. Consider, for example, a library circulation-control system. This will need forms to input barrier data, forms to note reservations, forms to notify borrowers of overdue items, forms to notify users of the availability of reserved items, to list only a few of the different types of forms necessary.

An organization that handles many different types of data, that necessitates the creation and maintenance of a number of different types of form, is well advised to appoint a forms controller. This may well be a full-time or more normally a part-time responsibility, depending on the magnitude of the task. The forms controller should be responsible for:

● The elimination of any unnecessary forms
● Periodic reviews of the forms that exist and the extent to which they meet the needs of the organization
● Control of the stockholding of printed forms
● Training and communication regarding efficient form completion and utilization.

With control exercised over these functions, the proliferation of forms should be eliminated, which should lead to fewer resources being devoted to the design, production, maintenance, completion, storage and utilization of forms. Forms are an important aspect of the interface between the system and the user, and effort directed towards effective forms control and design will be repaid.

Use of forms
Good forms are designed for the use for which they are intended. Forms can be used in input to and output from computer systems. They can also be used as data-storage devices in their own right. Here data may be entered onto a form, and the paper forms then stored, typically in some order. Originally, such form-filling systems were the major means of record-keeping within organizations. Today, most such systems supplement computer systems or are used for storage of data that are not regarded as worth entering into the database.

They may also be kept as a back-up security record of data in the database, or stored for accounting or other purposes.

Before embarking on the design of a form it is important to establish that the form serves one or several purposes that contribute to the objectives of the organization. In addition, the designer should ensure that there is no other form that serves or can be made to serve the same purposes, or with which the proposed form can be merged in order to serve their combined purposes easily or at a lower cost.

Input forms

The objective of an input form is to collect data from the points of origin of the data. These points of origin will be wherever transactions are taking place, or where new data to be entered into a database are being compiled. Such data may be created in a library in a cataloguing department, at a circulation-control desk or at an abstractor's desk. In other organizations the data may be created at a service point, on the factory floor, in an accounts department or in some other office department. These data-collection points may be within one building or on a number of sites, possibly scattered worldwide. In all instances the object of the form is to assist in the ready collection of accurate data.

On-screen forms facilitate the input of data directly into the database and will usually lead to immediate or relatively fast updating of the database so that records of new data and new transactions can be consulted very soon after they have been added to the database. Most such forms are likely to be completed by employees of the organization running the computer system or other trained users, although occasionally users from the wider public may be required to enter data on such forms.

Paper forms have been used for many years as a data-collection device. Originally the forms themselves were filed in order to store the data. Many such forms are now used to collect data for input into computer systems. These forms may be completed by a wide spectrum of people with differing levels of education, values and familiarity with the concepts covered by the form. Forms will normally be collated and data entered into a computer system by a key operator working at one of the keyboard-based input devices, and possibly using on-screen forms for this purpose. In this case it is important that the paper forms and on-screen forms are compatible with one another.

Output forms

An output form is a means of presenting data that are in the database in a form that is suitable for use. Forms may present numerical or statistical data and textual data. They are just one format of document that can be output from a computer system, and structured data of this kind may be integrated with graphics and text in a document. Output forms are typically designed for the output of data that are regularly printed out. Typical output forms in libraries are of issue statistics, forms concerning the availability of reserved items, overdue notices, and online public-access catalogue screens.

In situations where the system users have access to the computer system it is reasonable to present all output forms as a screen. These forms have the added advantage that once the data have been perused in the form in which they are initially presented they may be manipulated, changed and re-arranged to suit the user's requirements. In some cases the design of the form may be left to the user, and different users may have the same data, or subsets of the same data presented in different formats. Screen output does however assume that the user has access to a networked terminal. This is not always the case, especially if the user is a member of the general public or a member of, say, a professional body, rather than the employee of the organization running the computer system.

Paper output forms are useful where not all users have access to an appropriate terminal. They also have archival value. In addition they may be preferred by many users because they are easier to use. You can have a large paper form and examine different parts of the form or compare two pages side-by-side.

Since the strategy for the design of forms, and considerations relating to content and layout are common for paper and screen forms, these are discussed next.

Design stages

A list of the stages of form design may be useful in order to structure the process by which forms come into being. These stages might be:

- Define the objective of the form
- Specify the form's data content (the National Computing Centre Clerical-Document-Specification form may be used for this purpose)
- Decide upon the method of production of the form (e.g. on screen, or various printing methods)
- Design the form
- Review the draft form with the user
- Produce a fair specimen of the form
- Submit the form to the forms controller for approval
- Test the form
- Revise the form as necessary
- Implement the use of the form.

Content and layout of forms

In general the content should be decided in advance of the layout, but the two are related. The content of the form covers all words, spaces, lines, boxes etc. that appear on the form. A checklist of some of the points to remember is a useful starting-point.

1   *User needs*. The form must satisfy the needs of the person who is to complete it, and yet collect the data that are required by the system, in a form that the system can handle. For example, data to be entered into a database may need to be divided into fields. This imposes constraints on form design and upon the way in which the person completing the form is permitted to present data. This may be particularly restrictive if variable-length data have to be fitted into fixed-length fields. So inevitably forms will often reflect the database for which data are being collected and it is important also to make such forms amenable to the user.

2   *Appearance*. The form must in general be attractive to the eye and easy to follow with location of its specific parts being straightforward. Adherence to many of the guidelines that follow will contribute to an attractive form, but it is the way in which they are jointly applied that makes it attractive. Badly or inappropriately designed forms waste time and cause errors both in reading and interpretation and can lead to the input of inaccurate data.

3   *Logical sequencing*. The sequence in which information is presented or asked for should be logical in terms of the system itself and the activity being undertaken. For example, if data are being input for the creation of a catalogue record, the data should be required in an order which is similar to that in which the data can be expected to be encountered in the document being catalogued. The usual sequence of entry should follow the normal reading sequence. Where there are a number of users accessing the same system for different purposes, it may be necessary to compromise in form design. Here it is important that the user understands the sequence of the data and why they are ordered in the way that they are. In addition to sequencing of data, related data should be grouped. This enhances comprehension of labels etc. and permits users to complete all of the data relating to a specific item or aspect one after another. It may also reduce the space occupied by labels.

4   *Spaciousness*. Spacing and blanks are important in emphasizing the logical structure of the data. For example, greater spaces between blocks of relatively unrelated data can divide blocks of related data from one another. Adequate but not over-generous spacing also contributes to an appealing appearance. Attention needs to be directed to the allocation of adequate space for headings so that they are sufficiently prominent. Space allocated for information to be inserted needs to be sufficient but not over-generous, and should be related to the number of characters in an entry.

5   *Relevance* will contribute to logical sequencing and spaciousness. No irrelevant clutter should be shown on a form. There is always a temptation to collect too much information. Data which are only potentially relevant should not be collected, and should therefore not appear on the form.

6   *Consistency* in the language used in a form and across a set of forms designed for use by a group of users performing a set of related tasks is important.

7   *Language.* Any labels or explanations should be clear and brief without being overly brusque. Explanatory notes should be included where necessary, but these must be to the point.

8   *Titles, labels and entry headings* should be present, brief and clear. The form title must distinguish it from other forms for similar activities and should appear on each screen or page. This may need special attention where screen forms cover more than one screen. The labels or entry headings must guide the user as to the correct information to enter in each space. Labels must be close to the space to which they refer.

9   *Instructions for completion* must be kept to a minimum. Where they are necessary they should be seen before a person fills in the entry (and not at the foot of the page or screen). Pre-set options may be offered on the form so that the user is required merely to tick one of the options.

10   *Filing reference* must be included in an appropriate place on the form, if forms are to be filed in any sequence either during processing or in the longer term.

11   *Colour* can be an asset in form design, but it can be overdone. Paper forms are sometimes made in sets covering related information, but in different colours. This colour coding can be helpful in handling the forms. For printed forms it is usually the paper colour that may be varied, although it is possible to vary the ink colour as well. On a screen it is possible to vary both the background colour and the colour of the text on the form. Many weird and wonderful combinations are possible, but it is desirable to choose a combination that is legible, not nauseous, and restful to the eyes.

Paper forms – some special points

All of the points of design and content so far outlined apply equally well to paper and on-screen forms. There are, however, some points which relate specifically to paper forms and do not apply to screen forms. Paper forms must be printed and stored.

Printing

The main methods of printing available are:

(a) Letterpress printing, which is suitable for jobs where 10,000 or more high-quality copies are required. This would normally be performed by an external printer.

(b) Offset lithography is similar to letterpress, but a little cheaper, and more popular today. This method is economically viable if several thousand copies of a form are required.

(c) Offset duplicating may be used for smaller numbers of copies. A paper plate can be used to produce between 50 and 2,000 copies, a plastic plate up to 5,000 copies, and aluminium plates up to 25,000 copies.

(d) A photocopier may be used to produce small numbers of copies of forms.

The method chosen depends on:

- The number of copies of the form that are required
- The use to which the form is to be put
- The requirements as regards quality and appearance
- The time available for production of the form
- The acceptable cost of production of the form
- The printing facilities available within the organization.

Aspects of printing that need to be considered include:

- *Single- or double-sided printing*. Multi-sheet forms should be avoided if possible. However, double-sided forms are also more difficult to handle than one single-sided sheet.
- *Lines* should be used sparingly. Two distinct thicknesses is sufficient.
- *Typefaces*. A mixture of upper-case and lower-case, with the minimum number of different typefaces, is desirable.
- *Typesizes* selected depend on space available, user and user environment.
- *Colour* can be applied in the use of different-coloured papers or inks. However, unless colour has a distinct function, black and white is cheaper and easier.
- *Order quantity* depends on rate of usage, expected rate of modifications, shelf life and storage costs.

The masters for printing may be drawn on paper with pencil and ruler or may be designed with the aid of software for desktop publishing.

Paper
There are a number of considerations concerning the desirable characteristics of paper that need to be used with paper forms. Factors similar

to those which determine the optimum printing method also dictate aspects of the best paper for the job. Characteristics of paper to be considered include:

- *Size* should be sufficient to enter all of the entries. Paper is based on the A sizes, with A4 being the most common size, A5 half of A4 and A3 twice A4. It is best to opt for one of these standard sizes.
- *Surface quality*, in particular whether the paper is matt or polished.
- *Erasure characteristics*, for pencil, with typewriter and biro.
- *Weight and thickness*. Thicker, better-quality paper is heavier, and although it may stand more wear and tear, will be heavy to move, and occupy more storage space, both prior to use, and later in filing cabinets etc. if stored on a long-term basis. Weight is measured in grams per square metre (gsm). 49 gsm is normally used for typing copy paper and 61 gsm for normal letterheads and forms not subject to long-term handling.
- *Colour* may be used, but in addition to the factors above, the following should be considered:
  - problems arising from colour blindness of form users
  - fading
  - photocopying
  - printing costs of printing more than one colour ink
- *Construction*. Internal construction of paper determines its strength and capacity. It is not usually critical but where paper is used in high-speed equipment or subject to intensive handling strength may be important.

Design aspects

- Paper forms may be completed by typewriter or by hand. Entry spaces should allow appropriate space for typewritten or handwritten characters.
- Margins are necessary to allow for trimming after copying, and any holes that need to be punched for filing.
- Paper forms can be designed with the paper horizontal or vertical. It is usual to handle paper with the long side vertical. If the form is to be mailed using a window envelope this will influence layout.

Forms design is an important activity, since forms are central to the collection, transmission, interpretation, storage and retrieval of information. Forms make a significant contribution to system efficiency and effectiveness.

Codes and code design

Codes are widely used in computer systems. A code is a substitute for an item name. It has a number of functions, but its primary function is to make it possible to identify or retrieve coded items as efficiently as possible. The code may also group similar items together and summarize some of the properties of the item itself, such as price, accession date or how long it should be retained.

Many of the coding systems used in computer systems have derived from codes used by the organization prior to computerization and have their origins in the history of the organization. Nevertheless it is important to review any code that is currently in use from time to time. In addition, there will be occasions on which a new code is required, such as when:

- A new computer system is introduced
- The organization takes on additional functions
- The code can no longer be extended to cover other new items
- Two or more organizations with different coding systems merge, and a single code is needed.

Code design

In designing a code it is necessary to consider how that code is to be used. It is useful to consider:

- What the coded data are to be used for, and whether there is an optimum data sequence for this application
- What role the code plays in the use and arrangement of the data
- Who will use the code and how familiar they are likely to become with it
- The structure of the data and the file-management system
- The size of the file and whether hardware imposes any constraints on coding
- How frequently searching is performed
- The rate of growth of the file
- The role of the code outside the computer system, for example, whether it will also be used in various clerical routines.

Having taken these various factors into account, a code must be designed which has the following features.

Essential features of a code

- A code must be logically tailored to the system and the items to be coded. Many codes are based upon a classification, or systematic arrangement of the items to be coded, and may display the structure

of this classification
- There must be a unique code for each item
- The code should be as brief as is consistent with other constraints
- There should be scope for expansion and development to reflect changes in conditions, characteristics and relationships
- The structure of the code should be sufficiently clear, so that it is easy to apply
- A mnemonic code will facilitate clerical operations and retrieval
- The code must be compatible with the hardware and software and indexing systems with which it will be used
- The code should have a uniform size and format
- In many circumstances the code must be sortable, if records are likely to be listed in an order according to the code
- The code should be as stable as possible. Modifications are time-consuming and costly and should be avoided as far as possible.

Some examples of codes

The student of bibliographic classification schemes will already have encountered some well-known approaches to coding. In libraries a code is often also assigned to each borrower and each item in stock. A well-known code for books is the International Standard Book Number (ISBN), and for serials the International Standard Serial Number (ISSN). It is interesting to collect together all of the codes that you have been issued with as an entity in various systems. You are almost certain to have a bank-account code (possibly several), a National-Insurance number, an employee number or student number, a National-Health number, a tax-system number, a library-user code, a post code.

These codes are structured in different ways, as appropriate for the system of which they are part. Many are allocated so that numbers can be read by data-capture devices such as bar-code readers or magnetic-ink character-recognition devices, which need only to record a transaction against an appropriate user.

There are two basic types of codes: significant codes and non-significant codes. Significant codes contain some information concerning the entities they represent, e.g. St Law 1989, where this is the code for Staff (St) in the law department (Law), registered in 1989 (1989). Sequence codes are the main kind of non-significant code. The advantages of a non-significant code are that they are often shorter, easier to allocate, more flexible and less error-prone than the equivalent significant code.

Significant codes can be further divided into logical codes, such as self-checking codes, collating codes such as classification codes, and abbreviations.

All codes comprise letters, numbers and other characters such as punctuation marks. Codes should be a continuous string of characters. Letters from other alphabets, such as the Greek alphabet, are best avoided, as are most punctuation marks, the hyphen being one possible exception. Letters and numbers have a clear order. Codes may comprise upper-case and/or lower-case letters and/or numbers, i.e. they may be alphabetic, numeric, or alphanumeric.

Codes can be described as:

(a) *Sequence codes* involve the allocation of codes in order to a list of items, or the allocation of codes from a straight list as new items enter the system. Such codes are easy to allocate, but they reveal little about the relationships between the items in the system, and thus have no meaning and are difficult to remember. In addition, removal of old items from the system will lead to redundancy or some codes being unused.

   Block codes are a special kind of sequence code in which sequences are grouped within sequences or blocks. They assist in the memorization of codes for specific groups. All sections can be added to or deleted easily and the computer can carry out simple checks on code numbers during data input.

   Chronological codes are sequence codes where some time order is associated with the assignment of a particular code.

(b) *Self-checking codes.* Check characters or check digits may be appended to a code so that the computer can check that the code entered is acceptable and identify clerical errors. This character is derived from some mathematical technique involving all of the characters in the base code. There are a number of such techniques with various degrees of reliability. The most widely used is the 'modulus' check character. In this method each character in a code is multiplied by predetermined numbers (or weights); the check character is then the difference between the sum of these products and the next multiple of another predetermined number (the modulus). A good example of a self-checking code is the ISBN.

(c) *Classification codes.* Classification is the establishment of categories of entities and attributes in such a way that items that in some way are similar are brought together. Any classification scheme must be comprehensive, and contain mutually exclusive categories, so that there is only one place for every item. Classification usually involves the identification of classes and then sub-classes within those classes. The code assigned to a sub-class is usually unique only within a class, and may be re-used for sub-classes of other classes. The code for the sub-class is then a *Dependent code* since it depends for its uniqueness on the code for the main class.

A group classification code is where a number of related items are assigned grouped codes. For example, all bank accounts held at a certain branch have codes which start with the branch sorting code, e.g.

customer no. 1's code: 40-3366
customer no. 2's code: 40-3367

Such codes can be numerical or alphabetical. An alphabetical code has potentially 26 main groups, i.e. A, B, C, D . . . whereas a numerical code has only 10, i.e. 0, 1, 2, 3 . . . .

This means that an alphabetical coding system has greater capacity, and where all subdivisions are allocated is likely to lead to shorter codes. A simple hierarchical code is one where all items are arranged in order according to a particular characteristic, e.g. weight, thickness, age. In many systems a one-sequence hierarchical code is not appropriate, but the concept of hierarchies is incorporated into more complex classification systems.

In order to expand the capacity of a classification code decimal coding is often adopted. This coding was exploited to its full potential in the Dewey Decimal Classification Scheme. Sub-classes of items can be assigned an additional digit. This coding system has capacity for unlimited expansion, by merely extending the length of the code, and is logical and well structured. It can however lead to codes of varying lengths, which some software may have difficulty in handling. There are various methods for overcoming this problem, one of which is *blocking* the code to bring all codes up to a pre-specified length by filling in with 0s.

(d) *Mnemonic codes.* Another means of giving meaning to a code is to use letters or letters and numbers to represent the different characteristics or properties of the item being coded. The codes are designed to facilitate memorization of the codes. A code for a jigsaw puzzle, for example, might be:

W	100	70	60	A	LON
Wooden (the material)	Number of pieces	Width (cm)	Height (cm)	Adult (audience)	London (the subject)

These types of codes are particularly useful for stores parts, such as parts for machinery of various kinds. They are easy to change and to extend although it can be difficult to manage them for a large set of items. Codes such as the one above where a series of significant abbreviations are used together may be referred to as *facet* codes, since each piece of the total code describes a different facet or characteristic of the item. Each component of the code may be a sequence code or a group or a hierarchical classification code.

Such codes do have some drawbacks. In order to be able to recognize the logical structure of such codes it is necessary to have some means of knowing when a new facet is being introduced. This can be achieved by spaces, as in the example above, or by appropriate use of letters and numbers (e.g. a capital letter signals a new facet), or by allocating a set number of characters to each facet. Faceted codes are prone to become rather lengthy.

(e) *Alphabetic derived codes* are sometimes used in document indexing and in organizing files which handle many names and addresses. These codes are formed from the original alphabetic version of the title, name or address, or other textual label, and abbreviated to a code by the application of some standard set of rules. Examples of such rules might be: 'Remove all vowels from surnames', or 'Use initial letter of the name, followed by three digits formed from the 2nd, 3rd and 4th consonants'. These codes have the advantage that the computer can derive the code from the text presented to it, but such codes are inclined to lack uniqueness. For example, applying the first rule above would lead to the same codes being generated for Brown and Brawn. Some effort has been directed towards the design of rules that lead to greater uniqueness, but lack of uniqueness will always be an inherent problem with such codes.

Conclusion
The codes used by a system have an influence on data accuracy and effective retrieval of data. Although a major overhaul of the codes within an organization is rare, it is important that when such an exercise is undertaken it is performed with care and foresight.

Design and documentation of manual procedures
Typically the input of data to a computer system and the management of output from the system will generate associated clerical and manual procedures. For a typical online system, design of manual procedures must include consideration of all processes which emanate from or lead to points where the user interacts directly with the computer. In a batch system, manual procedures will often be more extensive, encompassing processes for preparation, batching and manual control of the data and arrangements for their transportation to and from input devices.

Manual procedures required to support the computer system need to be considered in outline very early in the project in order to estimate their cost and to assess their feasibility. However, detailed design and documentation is likely to be conducted towards the end of the project. The dataflow diagrams for the proposed system should facilitate the identification of those processes for which manual-procedure design is necessary. When designing clerical procedures it is important to take into account the physical environment, such as office layout and conditions, staffing and resource levels and the skills, knowledge and experience of system users.

Manual procedures should be documented and presented to the user as part of a system specification or manual. This document should include:

- *Introduction* to the system, and its objectives
- *Procedure specifications*, to describe the clerical procedures within the system
- *Data*, giving samples of input and output documents and displays, specification of new clerical files and a description of computer-based data files
- *Supporting information* showing responsibilities for the new system, and specific subsystems
- *Changeover*, dealing with the transition from existing to new procedures, timescales, critical activities, deadlines and workloads.

Documentation

Documentation can be divided into three broad categories:

- *Project documentation*, which is produced as the result of various stages in the analysis, design or implementation process. With a large project there may be a large quantity of such documentation, and it is important that this be appropriately organized and stored for reference at a later date
- *System technical documentation*, which explains the structure and internal workings of the system and may be produced at different levels of complexity for system-support programmers and expert users
- *User-operations manual*, which gives instructions on how to use the system. User manuals must be clear, concise and well structured. Users have two kinds of requirements of documentation: *education*, to find out about the system and how to operate it in its early stages of implementation; and *reminder*, to access a specific piece of information quickly, and often in an emergency. These are conflicting demands, the first requiring a well-structured guide, the second requiring direct access to a specific point.

These conflicting requirements can most helpfully be met by writing a number of separate documents, which may include:

- A quick-training guide for users who do not have sufficient time to read a more thorough account, and, anyway, need to learn only about the basic features of the system
- A more thorough guide for users who need to investigate all aspects of the system, which leads users through the various facets of the system one at a time
- A reference guide, possibly organized according to commands or functions, which includes all of the features of the system and is thoroughly indexed
- A quick-reference card of essential commands or functions.

These documents may be supported by or incorporated into an on-screen 'help' system.

The documentation to be produced for a given application must depend on the user group. Nevertheless, some general guidelines apply to all documentation:

1. Structure information in a hierarchical manner, using chapters, sections, paragraphs etc.
2. Label these sections with clear headings and numbering to show relationships.
3. Paragraphs and sentences should be short and to the point.
4. Instructions and text should be jargon free.
5. Procedures should be laid out sequentially and numbered to show the steps.
6. Important steps should be highlighted, using bold characters, different fonts or icons.
7. Use pictures, diagrams and visual methods to illustrate points if possible.
8. Keywords should be placed in the margin to provide direct access to specific topics.
9. Point-by-point summaries should be given at the ends of chapters.

Conclusion

This chapter has reviewed aspects related to the design of the human — computer interface, focusing on how people should design computer systems to make them work for them. In some environments encountered by the information professional a good number of these parameters may be fixed. For example, there may or may not be opportunity to influence dialogue design. It may not be necessary to pass rigorously through a stage of input-item definition, but on the other hand output-item definition may be a useful exercise.

Where a software package or turnkey system is being installed the scope to design the human−computer interface may be relatively limited. In this case, this chapter may act as a guide to the evaluation of the human−computer interface in systems under evaluation.

The options available for the design of the human−computer interface are mushrooming with the advent of new technological developments. Yet we still need to know more about users and how they interact with computers. The design of the interface is crucial, and interfaces must cater for the characteristics and needs of the intended users.

Further reading

Booth, P. A., *An introduction to human−computer interaction*, Hove, Erlbaum, 1989.

Mark, A. (ed.), *Fundamentals of human−computer interaction*, London, Academic Press, 1985.

Sutcliffe, A., *Human−computer interface design*, Basingstoke, Macmillan, 1988.

Winfield, I., *Human resources and computing*, London, Heinemann, 1986.

Chapter Five

Implementation of computer systems

Introduction
The implementation phase of a systems-analysis-and-design exercise is
concerned with getting a system operational. This phase involves much
the same processes for any system, whether a tailor-made system for
a specific application or a turnkey system or software package is being
implemented. A little more testing may be necessary with a new package,
but providing the earlier stages of the project have been effectively
completed, additional problems should be minimal.

Figure 5.1 summarizes the stages in the implementation phase of the
project. It concludes, as does this chapter, with systems review and
evaluation. This has been earlier defined as a separate phase, which
indeed it is, but it is a necessary component of successful implementation. Review and evaluation, like control and security, have been drawn
into this chapter for convenience. They are both related to the operational
system.

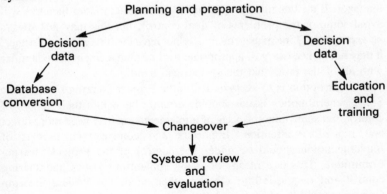

Fig. 5.1   Stages in the implementation phase of a systems-analysis-and-
design project

Planning and preparation

The first stage of implementation must be planning and preparation. This includes responsibility for site preparation, and hardware and software installation. Education and training and plans for security are also part of the preparation for systems implementation.

Planning and preparation are crucial to successful implementation. Planning for implementation should be part of the design stage of the system. Nevertheless, just prior to implementation it will be necessary to review these plans. This is the stage at which the system starts to affect the whole organization. Prior to this stage it has been primarily the concern of the systems analyst, the Project Management Team and the Project Steering Committee. The implementation of the system may involve disruptions to working practices, challenges to users and possible management and trade-union problems. The number of people concerned with the system on a day-to-day basis suddenly escalates once it moves from design to implementation.

Control

Priority must be accorded to consideration of control of implementation. A delicate balance must be achieved. Control can be split between the systems analyst and the line management or departmental manager. It is important that the systems analyst's role is maintained as that of trainer and adviser and that the line management's authority is not challenged. This requires careful liaison between the systems analyst and line manager. The objective is to avoid a situation where the line manager says one thing should be done, and the systems analyst says or appears to say something which conflicts with instructions issued by the line manager. If the line manager can act as adviser and trainer then this will avoid some of the problems of dual control, but this may not always be appropriate. Line management may not have the time to train. Further, it may not be necessary or appropriate for line management to be familiar with all of the tasks that the system can handle.

Another option is to vest control in the Project Steering Committee. Some general-policy issues should certainly be within their sphere of control, but some minor aspects of implementation may need more direct and immediate attention. Important and controversial aspects of implementation should be under the control of the Project Steering Committee. This is a means of airing contentious issues and sharing control and responsibility. On the other hand, the Project Steering Committee will be slow to make decisions. A decision must await the next committee meeting. Its effectiveness may depend on the chairperson and the frequency of meetings. Again the Project Steering Committee can, if it exerts its control inappropriately, undermine the control of line management.

Site preparation

The extent of site-preparation measures will depend on the scale of the system. Typical areas that need to be considered are:

1 *Power supply*. Although smaller computers may use the ordinary mains power supply, it is still necessary to check whether there are sufficient power outlets and adequate circuit capacity. Two or more circuits make the system more reliable, should there be any problems with one of the circuits. Also, it is necessary to ensure that the computer equipment will not be adversely affected by surges on circuits caused by other electrical equipment. Large machines may need their own dedicated power supplies, with stand-by generators to cater for power cuts.

2 *Air conditioning*. Smaller computers do not normally need air conditioning, but on hot days sun coming in through windows may overheat the equipment. It is therefore wise to consider carefully the siting of equipment so that it is not vulnerable to overheating. Larger machines need a full air-conditioning system, which should be installed as part of the office alterations.

3 *Site alterations*. Sometimes a computer system is installed as part of the construction of a new building. If an existing building is being used alterations may be necessary as a result of:

- The space required for a new large computer system
- Accommodation for terminals, such as on a library issue desk, or at another service point
- Company reorganization
- Air-conditioning requirements
- Circuiting requirements
- Necessary modifications to workplace layout.

It is important that all site alterations are complete before the equipment arrives. They can be executed more easily without equipment on site, and the dust that such alterations generate will not do the equipment any good!

4 *Office equipment*. A new computer system often heralds unimagined requirements for new office furniture. Now that the personal computer is a standard element of office equipment each person needs two desks instead of one − one for the computer and one for paper! Terminals certainly need working space, often in the form of a desk. There may

be special desk requirements. Chairs and desks need to be selected with ergonomic considerations in mind.

New equipment

The implementation of the computer system will necessitate the acquisition of various equipment. Apart from the obvious hardware and software, telecommunications links may need to be installed, and arrangements may need to be made for various more minor supplies, such as paper and printer ribbons.

1 *Hardware.* If a large installation is being planned a variety of different kinds of hardware will be acquired ranging from the central processor or computer itself, to disc drives, printers and terminals. Some of this equipment may be acquired from different suppliers. Different equipment may have different supply times. Orders need to be placed in such a way that equipment arrives when it is required. It is most important to avoid serious delays in delivery times of crucial pieces of equipment.

2 *Software.* In general software, if it is available on the market as a completed package, will have a short delivery time. Once the software is acquired it is important to check once again that it runs satisfactorily on the hardware configuration.

3 *Telecommunications.* The supply of telecommunications circuits is often subject to a long delay. It is therefore important to establish circuit requirements early, and to take any likely delays in the supply of telecommunications lines into account in any implementation schedule.

4 *Supplies.* The variety of ancillary equipment and supplies that may be necessary to support a computer system will vary with the system. It may include tapes, discs, tape racks, racks or shelves for system documentation and many other similar items. Printers need stationery. It will be necessary to establish or estimate:

- The first order quantity
- The re-order quantity
- Likely usage
- Period between orders
- Paper specification, e.g. quality, number of parts, layout.

Orders need also to be placed for any pre-printed stationery. The layout should already have been agreed at the design stage. Here it is a matter of making arrangements for printing.

System testing

System testing is conducted in order to ensure that the system works effectively before it goes into full implementation. Preliminary testing should ensure that hardware and software work independently, and then together. Testing must be exhaustive. Since considerable time may have elapsed since the original analysis, volumes of data and transactions, and work practices should be reviewed, and any appropriate modifications made to the system. As many minor system modifications as possible should be executed prior to exposing the system to users, as such modifications can be confusing and frustrating for them. Once the systems analyst is confident that the system will work, operational trials can be conducted. These should involve users, since they must test people and their training as well as the system.

System trials will need to be based on *test data*. This test data will be designed to test key areas of the system; exhaustive testing would often be too time-consuming. Clearly those parts of the system that will be used frequently must be tested thoroughly, as will any systems procedures where an error or failure would be disastrous. Any trial should take place in an environment which is as close as possible to the real one.

All facets of the system must be checked. A program which covers most aspects of the system must be drafted. Typical areas for attention are:

(a) *Inputs testing* to cover:
   - forms design
   - data transmission
   - data preparation and controls
   - computer-input validation including item formats, combinations and sequence
   - submission of corrections.

(b) *File testing* includes:
   - validity of format
   - ease of maintenance
   - ease of updating
   - ease of storing
   - file security
   - testing for each type of transaction
   - tests for no transactions
   - at least one of every reportable error and exception
   - production of every type of output.

(c) *Outputs testing* must include:
- forms design
- completion and ease of preparation
- controls and transmission
- understanding by the recipient
- use of VDUs
- each type of report
- production of summary reports
- paper handling, especially at ends of pages
- use of pre-printed stationery.

(d) *Computer procedures testing* including:
- program linkages
- operating procedures
- recovery and security
- response times
- effect on other computers and other systems.

(e) *Clerical procedures*, for example:
- understanding of the user documentation, help systems etc.
- error-correction procedures
- information flow and response time for outputs
- staffing, supervision, capacities, office layout and equipment
- audit requirements and controls.

System test data and test results should be preserved as a *test log*. The test log is part of the systems documentation and should be kept for the life of the system so that it is available for later reference.

Once thorough trials of the hardware, software and people have been completed, the system needs to be set up for any data conversion.

Data conversion

Master copies must be set up to support the system. For example, a library circulation-control system cannot function without a file of borrower details and a file of details of stock. The creation of such files may be extremely time-consuming and an estimate must be made of the work involved in the creation of such files at an early stage. Devon Library Services, like many public and academic libraries, took advantage of Manpower Services Commission staff to convert the records of 2.25 million items of stock, and 400,000 titles to machine-readable form. Between 1986 and March 1988, over 100 staff had been involved in this process. A further 50 staff were expected to complete the process during

1988. It is clear that a process on this scale needs careful management and control. Decisions need to be made concerning how existing databases are to be converted, by whom, and over what timescale.

Existing data may be in manual or computer files. If data are to be transferred from manual files careful conversion procedures need to be established, especially as the data conversion may be performed by relatively inexperienced clerical staff. Access to the data may be difficult if, as with a card catalogue, for instance, it is normally in use elsewhere. Problems associated with access need to be resolved. Another problem arises from the accuracy of existing records. Catalogue records, for example, may inaccurately reflect the current stock situation, and/or the data recorded in them may reflect earlier cataloguing practices, and may need updating.

Conversion of a card catalogue into machine-readable form, for instance, may involve elimination of entries for books no longer in stock, and the imposition of consistent cataloguing and classification practices on a set of catalogue records that has passed through many cataloguers' hands over an extended period of time. Another distinction to be made is between static and dynamic data. Static data, such as details of books in stock, may be keyed well ahead of changeover, whilst dynamic data, such as who has which book on loan, may not be transferred until shortly before changeover, or even during changeover.

Conversion from a manual file to a computer-based file can be a mammoth task. Many computerized library-housekeeping systems go live before complete conversion has been achieved. For example, records for all recent books may be added to the catalogue database prior to changeover, whilst records for older items may be added only when that particular item passes through the issue desk.

Boss recommends that libraries with fewer than 500,000 volumes have machine-readable records for at least 50% of their holdings before implementing a computer system, and that larger libraries should have machine-readable records for at least the past five years' acquisitions.

There are three major means of retrospective conversion of bibliographic records, a major problem for libraries with established collections where full bibliographic records have not been machine-readable in the past:

(a) Conversion and upgrading of records as and when they are being used for some other purpose. This has the advantage of avoiding a major conversion project but may interfere with other routines, and it will be a long time before all the file is converted.

(b) Selection of records from large bibliographical databases available from commercial vendors. This is unlikely to cover all the records that are in need of conversion, but may cater for a substantial proportion of the database.

(c) Send records to a data conversion agency. This may be expensive, but offers greater quality control, and faster conversion.

File set-up

Once the data have been converted into machine-readable form, the files must be set up for the new system. Usually the normal programs for handling master-file additions will be used, but sometimes special programs may be necessary. A major concern during file set-up is accuracy and error detection and correction. Errors can be detected by computer checking or clerical checking. Computer checking is fast and can check consistency of data, completeness and reasonableness. Clerical checking of print-out against original documents should provide a comprehensive check on accuracy, but it is labour-intensive (and boring!). Clearly, once errors are detected, there needs to be a procedure for their correction.

Education and training

Education and training is an important element of successful implementation. However good the system is, without commitment on the part of its users, be they staff of an organization or its customers, it will not operate as planned. Users must be convinced of the benefits of the new system, both to themselves and to the organization. The other objective of education and training is to ensure that users understand their own role in the new system, and that they are competent in completing specific tasks. Education and training are complementary but distinct activities.

Education

Education is a pre-requisite to training. Everyone who performs tasks which lie in the domain of change needs education. Education focuses on a general awareness of the system and its benefits. One of its primary roles is to convince the user of the benefits of the system. Appropriate attitudes are a prerequisite to successful training. Education must eliminate fear and misunderstandings and must start early in the development of the system. Nevertheless, education needs a special focus during the implementation of the system. Early education is concerned with the creation of the feeling of involvement, and should include sessions which create an atmosphere in which users are at ease to discuss and air their reservations and apprehensions. Education should contribute towards dissipating resistance.

Staff training

The aim of training is to give staff the specific skills required in their use of the system. Training should contain as much hands-on work as possible. Users need to be made familiar with the system and the documentation. It can be difficult to schedule training. Spare staff capacity is unusual and training takes time. It is entirely unrealistic to expect to be able to train the complete staff at one session, since probably only one or two members of staff will be released to training at any given moment. Training will therefore need to be conducted with one or two people or in small groups, and is likely therefore to absorb a considerable amount of the trainer's time. Another constraint on the scheduling of training is availability of terminals, especially prior to or during implementation of the system. A training programme may assist in the recognition and reduction of some of these problems.

The training programme must be planned and scheduled. All staff must become proficient in the operation of the system before it is introduced. A progressive build-up of knowledge for each individual is the easiest way of learning. The training programme will be determined by:

- Aims of the training programme
- Resources available for training
- Staff selected for training
- Extent of training
- Time available for training.

It is important to draw up a training schedule.

Training sessions must be short and frequent. They should briefly explain:

- Why a task is being performed
- What is being accomplished in terms of the overall system
- How the task should be carried out.

Sessions must be tailored to the requirements of individual staff.

Timing of training sessions can be crucial. Sessions that are too early will be forgotten before the system is implemented. On the other hand, if the training sessions are left too late, and training is rushed prior to implementation, users may flounder if required to absorb too much at once. Also, training sessions are an opportunity to assess from a number of people's viewpoints the effectiveness of the system. Training sessions may provide information on necessary minor refinements of the system. If training sessions are too late, then there may not be time for incorporating these minor changes into the system.

Learning difficulties that arise during training are the responsibility of the trainer and the systems analyst, not the system user. Indeed, one might go further and assert that the better system will stand alone, with the minimum of training.

Training is an on-going activity. Whilst a significant effort must be invested in training immediately prior to implementation, staff turnover will lead to a need for an on-going training programme for new staff, and staff whose role in relation to the system changes. Much of this on-going programme must comprise on-the-job training by experienced staff. It is therefore all the more important that user manuals are good, and that experienced staff have a sound appreciation of the system, which is likely to have developed from their own initial training. Often it is useful if one particular member of staff is responsible for the coordination of training. It is also necessary to recognize that on occasions re-training of existing staff who have forgotten, or slipped into bad habits may be appropriate.

Training methods may be one of or a mixture of the following teaching and learning methods. Each method has its own particular strengths:

(a) *Lectures* are useful to explain background, philosophy, the general structure of the system, and generally to convey information. They are particularly appropriate with larger groups.

Twelve tips for effective lectures

1 The audience's attention will wander. Use audio-visual aids.
2 Sessions should not exceed 30 to 50 minutes.
3 Make the content clear, structuring and grouping ideas as appropriate.
4 Don't talk too fast. Repeat yourself from time to time to emphasize points.
5 Observe whether the audience is taking notes, and adjust the speed of lecturing accordingly.
6 Watch the audience, in particular their faces and hands.
7 Encourage questions and don't put people down or make them feel small or inadequate for asking even the most trivial or idiotic questions.
8 Check the legibility of any audio-visual aids, especially blackboards and overhead-projector slides.
9 Make sure the audience can hear at the back.
10 Don't walk up and down in front of the board.
11 Tell them what you're going to tell them, tell them, and then tell them what you have told them.

12 Start with objectives for the session, and do your best to build in some mechanism for checking that these objectives have been achieved.

(b) *Seminars and discussion groups* are less formal than lectures. There should be ample opportunity for participants to discuss their viewpoints, and to share ideas. In order that everybody has the opportunity to talk and listen in such groups, group sizes should ideally be between four and ten people.

Ten tips for effective seminars or discussion groups

1 Make sure that the participants participate.
2 Discussion will need directing. It is necessary to start with objectives and, if appropriate, to explain these objectives to the group.
3 If they won't talk give them something to do and get them to report back. This is effective if the group is split into twos or threes to discuss an issue or to complete a task.
4 Remember that participants learn as much, if not more, from one another as from the trainer. Strive to create an environment in which this is possible.
5 Learn to shut up and encourage others to have their say, even if they aren't as knowledgeable or wise as you.
6 Leave the room if you feel your presence inhibits discussion or completion of the task.
7 Give appropriate guidance and information willingly, cheerfully, and without being patronizing, when asked.
8 Give the group time to sort itself out, but if it is clear that it is floundering, assist.
9 Be conscious of difficult individuals and ensure that they do not take control of the group. Ideally the group should control itself, with participants contributing to discussion and decisions. If this cannot be achieved, then the trainer must control the group in preference to an unacceptable group member.
10 Close the seminar with a summary of what the group has achieved, and how this contributes to the overall training objectives.

(c) *Online tutorials.* Many systems that are widely used by a large number of different people will be supported by an online tutorial. All of the better-known microcomputer software packages, for example, are supported by an online tutorial. This tutorial will take the user systematically through the various features of the system.

The best tutorials are interactive in that each feature is introduced, and the user is then able to experiment with that feature. Such tutorials vary considerably in quality and approach, but should be suitable for individual study. However, the learner needs a certain level of motivation and confidence to work through an online tutorial without any support.

(d) *Workshops* can take on a variety of different forms. The implication in the name workshop is that participants are going to do something. Typically a workshop will be run by a tutor, who is working with a group of say four to twelve people. The tutor will have a role in explaining the tasks that the participants are to complete, giving background information, offering advice and support and generally managing the environment. The participants will normally be given a task to complete or some objectives to achieve and be expected either individually or as a group or series of groups to work towards those objectives. When workshops are used as a training method prior to the implementation of a computer system, the tasks to be completed are likely to simulate aspects of the way in which this particular group can be expected to make use of computer systems. Workshops can be particularly useful in allowing the participants to lend each other support in learning and in exchange of ideas on practical aspects of systems use.

(e) *On-screen help facilities* are help facilities that are embedded in the system, and can be called up by the user at various stages during the use of the system. Most reputable systems should have some on-screen help facilities. As distinct from other methods of training discussed here they are designed primarily for on-the-spot problem-solving. For example, they answer questions such as 'How do I delete a field?' or 'What is the truncation symbol?' As such they are a feature of the human–computer interface, and are discussed more fully in Chapter Three.

(f) *User manuals* should form part of every system. Usually such manuals will be printed, but some part of them may also, or alternatively, be available on-screen, and may form part of the on-screen help facilities. User manuals should explain to the user how to perform all the functions that it is anticipated that the user may wish to perform with the system. As a means of training, manuals usually lack dynamism and direction and may be difficult to get started with. However, some manuals that have been carefully constructed with special introductory exercises followed by a more complete review of system features can be used as an introduction to the software. In many circumstances, manuals will be the only training available to the potential user, and they need to be designed with the first-time user in view. Nevertheless, the essential function of a manual is as a reference tool for the experienced user. User manuals are discussed in more detail in Chapter Three since they represent part of the human—computer interface.

User education
In a situation where a computer system is to be used by customers and users as well as staff of the organization, strategies for user education need to be considered alongside those for staff education and training. This is the case, for instance, where an OPAC is being introduced into a library, or where a CD-ROM product is being made available to users.

There are a variety of different opinions on the need for and the form of user education in libraries. In relation, for example, to computerized systems there is a view that the user should not need education or training.

The first problem in planning any programme of user education is the identification of the users.

User education may and should take a variety of different forms. Users have different learning styles and so a variety of instructional methods is useful. These may include:

- Lectures
- Workshops
- Seminars
- Online help systems
- Online tutorials
- Diagnostic error messages
- Labelling of menus etc.

Any user-education programme should be evaluated. Evaluation should contribute towards plans for an improved programme as well as provide data on which a case for additional resources can be based.

Promoting the new system
An adjunct to an effective staff- and user-training programme is the promotion of a positive image of the new system and the effect that the system may have on an organization as a whole. Appropriate mechanisms for such promotion will depend on the system and its context, but might include:

- Leaflets describing the new system
- Newsletters or inserts in staff or user bulletins
- Displays

- Demonstrations
- Media stories
- Effective strategies for remedial activity when the system mal-
  functions.

The changeover — going live

The changeover can be defined as the period between the start of full
running of the new system, and the withdrawal of special support from
the systems analyst, designer, suppliers etc., other than the normal
maintenance support.

Devon Library Services, for example, during implementation expected
the supplier to be responsible in all respects for the good health of the
system. In the event of a problem, Devon simply had to call one number
and leave it to the service desk to sort out the problem. Once fully
operational the system had to be suitable for control by clerical staff.

There are three main strategies for changeover: switchover, parallel
running, and phased introduction.

(a) *Switchover* is the complete replacement of the old system with a
    new one. Switchover is risky, in the sense that everything depends
    on the new system. Where essential data are being recorded or there
    is an interface with the public, direct switchover can be particularly
    risky.

    The main attraction of direct switchover is that it removes the
    need to run two systems in parallel, which can be time-consuming
    and introduces additional complexities into working practices.
    Successful switchover depends heavily upon a thoroughly tested
    system, both in terms of the system itself and the system users. Prior
    to the start of a switchover, the consequences of any problems must
    be considered, contingency plans made, and staff briefed.

(b) *Parallel running* involves running both old and new systems in
    parallel, and then cross-checking the results. Parallel running does
    offer an opportunity for a fully operational run of the new system
    without placing full reliance upon it. However it does require the
    resources, including people, machines, accommodation and all other
    system resources, to support both systems simultaneously. Parallel
    running can only be an intermediate phase of limited duration since
    eventually the new system must replace the old.

(c) *Phased introduction* of the system involves introducing the system
    gradually. It starts with pilot-running.

    Pilot-running involves one of:

- Implementing only specified modules in the system, e.g. cataloguing, ordering
- Implementing the full system in selected departments or at chosen points
- Implementing a system based on only part of the file, e.g. all orders placed for maps, current-awareness profiles for a given department.

Pilot-running offers staged introduction of the system and yet should simulate all features of the running of the full system. On the other hand, the system that is being run is smaller than the full system, and involves fewer people and can therefore be controlled and monitored more readily.

It is important, however, that a self-contained unit of operation or file can be identified for pilot-running, otherwise users may be confused as to which system applies. Also, the pilot-run should be as representative as possible of the full system. Once a successful pilot-run has been completed and evaluated, other parts of the system may be introduced gradually. An ideal environment in which to use phased introduction and pilot-running is in the introduction of a library circulation-control system in a public library. It is easier to manage the introduction of the system to one branch at a time. In Devon Library Authority, for example, during the implementation of their new catalogue system a pilot branch, St Thomas at Exeter, went live in 1985, and a further 20 branches went live in April 1987. During 1988 it was planned that another 15 branches should also go online. In the near future it is planned to implement a relational database provided by the DS Galaxy system, which will link the full catalogue and circulation-control systems. This will be followed by the implementation of the Galaxy acquisition module, and systems for budgetary control, commitment control, payment authorization, service-level forecasting and auto-restocking. This demonstrates the use of phased introduction in a public-library authority, and is typical of the way in which many libraries approach computerization or the upgrade of their computer-based systems.

Security

It is important that computer hardware, software and databases remain secure. Considerable effort and cost are directed towards the construction of computer systems and databases. All of these efforts can be sabotaged if hardware is stolen, databases are corrupted or some other mishap afflicts the system. It is therefore important to attend to the security of computer systems and to develop a security policy.

The loss of security arises from accidental and deliberate threats. Accidental threats include a poor system, carelessness and errors. Deliberate threats arise from human intent and include theft, computer fraud, vandalism, and attempts to break the system. Typically such threats may lead to:

- The interruption of data preparation and data input
- The destruction or corruption of stored data
- The destruction or corruption of software
- The disclosure of personal or proprietary information
- Injury to personnel
- Removal of equipment or information.

In general the consequences of loss of security are loss of:

- Availability of the system — the system or data are not operational when required
- Integrity of the system — the system doesn't perform as required
- Confidentiality of the system — control of access to the system is not maintained.

Security policies

Any organization which uses computer systems needs a security policy to minimize the occurrence of loss of security and the effects of any loss of security. Such a security policy must:

- Identify the risks to which the system is exposed
- Assess the probability of each threat occurring and the consequences of a given threat
- Select counter-measures for threats on the basis of effectiveness, cost and security demands
- Outline contingency measures to tackle situations where loss of security is unavoidable.

These arrangements must be monitored and periodically reviewed. Any security policy must be drafted in cooperation with senior management, and must take into account any difficulties that security measures may present for system users. A security policy must be a locally designed policy which caters for local circumstances and environments and its implications and requirements need to be fully appreciated by any people who have access to the system who might inadvertently jeopardize its security. Data security is often in the hands of keyboard operators, and hardware security in the hands of computer technicians, maintenance

staff and even users. The security policy should be clearly recorded in
a written document and communicated and enforced as appropriate. The
elements of the security policy will repay further discussion. These are:

1 *Risk identification.* All elements of the system should be regarded
as potentially at risk, although inevitably some elements are more at risk
than others. These include, most obviously, the hardware and software
and the data in the system. They also include communications and aspects
of the wider environment. For example, a power cut in the building which
houses the system centre can be disastrous. Organizational changes, such
as change in management policy and structure and changes in personnel,
may also affect system security. Changes in system support, such as
maintenance arrangements, may also affect the system security. Each
element of the system should be considered, and the type of risk to which
it is exposed needs to be assessed, and the causes of those risks identified.

Once risks have been identified it is important to assess the losses that
may be incurred if breaches in security arise. Losses fall into a number
of categories:

- Property losses, e.g. loss of equipment
- Liability losses, e.g. breach of contract, contravention of copyright
- Personnel losses, e.g. death, injury, industrial action, resignation,
  leave of absence
- Financial losses, e.g. bad debts, dishonest employees
- Business interruption losses, e.g. delayed cash flows, increased
  cost of working.

It is preferable to be able to measure risks or to express them on some
scale so that it is possible to compare the various risks and to identify
those that should be considered most carefully. One means of doing this
is to express expected loss in monetary terms. This may not always be
possible.

2 *Counter-measures* are used to handle risks. Counter-measures
should make the system more secure and reduce the incidence of the
loss of security. Counter-measures can involve many different
approaches, but can be grouped into four different categories:

- Avoidance of risks, by for instance, changing procedures that involve
  risks to security
- Retention of risks, where the risks are either minor, or, although
  more major, judged to be too expensive or difficult to control
- Reduction of risks, such as by access control
- Transfer of risks, by for instance insurance cover or maintenance
  contracts so that if a breach in security arises the loss is borne by

someone else, such as the insurance company.

Counter-measures need to be considered in all areas where risks arise. In selecting any specific counter-measure it is necessary to consider:

● Its cost
● Any expected loss
● The effectiveness of the counter-measure in reducing frequency and/or the impact of the risk.

The counter-measures must be selected on the basis of cost effectiveness, and evaluated in the light of any expected loss.

3 *Contingency planning.* Even with an effective set of counter-measures, from time to time a risk will arise for which no adequate counter-measure has been applied. Such situations may arise when it has been deliberately decided to retain risks or when a risk arises which was not originally identified. Most systems will, occasionally, be subject to breaches of security, and appropriate contingency plans are necessary. Whilst contingency plans are necessary, they are often difficult to formulate. This is because it is difficult to predict when a breach of security will occur, and the action to be taken depends upon:

● The nature of the interruption
● The nature of the computer-based system which has been interrupted
● The expected duration of the interruption
● The damage caused by the interruption.

A security audit which maintains records of any security problems can be useful in formulating contingency plans as it can help in identifying the kinds of breaches of security that are likely to be encountered.

One component of contingency planning must be a strategy for systems recovery. The stages of systems recovery are:

(a) Identifying the system failure. A system failure may be recognized by wrong output, the computer detecting a fault, or the system operating with a reduced level of service
(b) Determining the type of failure, including locating fault and discovering the extent of damage to files, software and equipment
(c) Getting the system working as soon as possible, whilst
(d) Rectifying the fault
(e) Correcting all damage
(f) Restoring normal service.

Availability of computer systems
We have considered the security of computer systems in general terms.

In order to be more specific about risks and their counter-measures it is useful to focus attention on specific types of risks. One major area of concern is to maintain the availability of any system.

Physical security is the most basic requirement if the system is to remain available. Risks that may be encountered include:

- Inability to access terminals due to fire, flood, picketing and other damage
- Hardware failure and theft
- Electricity failure
- Telecommunications failure
- Failure of data and software.

Counter-measures for most of these risks involve making stand-by or duplicate facilities available. For hardware failure, such stand-by facilities should be at a different site. A good example of stand-by facilities is the ability to record transaction data locally and to read these data into the system when the main system is again operational. Such a system is common in library circulation-control systems.

File integrity and data corruption will be considered more fully in the next section.

Appropriate counter-measures for risks to physical security tend to revolve around access control. Personnel can engage in both accidental and deliberate loss. During an industrial dispute, for example, magnetic tapes containing crucial data may be removed. Accidental overwriting of data on tape is not as rare as it should be. Some counter-measures that contribute to effective access control include:

(a) Control of documentation, working papers, etc. such that these are available only to known individuals and are locked away when not in use. Records should be kept of the whereabouts of each copy of documentation.

(b) Control of access to hardware installations or environments where terminals are in use. Options here include:

- Manual signing-in of visitors
- Mechanical door locks (although problems with keys inevitably ensue!)
- Electronic systems using cards.

Hardware is less vulnerable to loss or theft if it is heavy and bulky. Portable microcomputers, for example, are vulnerable in most environments. Floppy discs are very easy to lose amongst a heap of papers. Terminals and microcomputers can be bolted to desks, in order to improve their security, although this will not prevent on-site vandalism.

(c) Access control to the data in the systems through passwords and user IDs, and data encryption. There is a wide variety of different levels of sophistication to password-access systems. Simple systems merely provide access to the system. An elementary improvement is to permit some passwords to allow the user to read only, whilst others may write and read. Other systems discriminate between files, or parts of files and records, or parts of records to which a given user may be permitted access, and may discriminate between read and write access for these various data items.

(d) A variety of other measures, such as good industrial relations, appropriate fire regulations, and effective plumbing that doesn't cause floods.

All security measures must, by their very nature, pose a barrier to access. It is important that these barriers do not become too intrusive, and equally important that they cannot be side-stepped or forgotten.

Security and integrity of files
Another major area to consider in a security policy is the security of files. It is necessary to keep the data accurate and the files complete, and to avoid unauthorized use. There are four components of the data-handling process which are subject to breaches in security:

● Input
● Files
● Processing
● Output.

Each of these areas needs to be considered in turn.

Input
The creation or amendment of records needs to be most carefully monitored if:

● Input is decentralized and performed by a large number of different people
● Input is first recorded on paper, and then keyed into the system.

Some data are more important than others, and therefore need to be monitored more carefully. For example, financial data usually need to be accurate. The mistyping of one character can be disastrous, whereas the mistyping of one character in a title or an item description will not lead to the same kind of calamity. Mistyping of textual material is most likely to hinder appropriate filing and subsequent retrieval of a record, but will not affect cumulative totals.

Input must be received, authorized, keyed and processed. Data control must know what kind of records to expect and their normal volume. There must be control over the authorization of input. There must be some mechanism for checking the records added to the system, either by printing out new and amended records or by scanning the records on the screen. This checking can be tedious but is necessary for accurate files. Responsibility for checking must be in the hands of specified individuals.

File security
Once data have been input to the system it is necessary to keep those data secure.

Physical security is the first factor to consider. Master copies must be made and kept in an environment in which they are safe from fire, theft, heat, stray magnetic and electrical fields and inadvertent loss. Other copies of files also need to be kept safely. Records should be maintained on the movement of files, and tapes and discs must be appropriately labelled. Instructions concerning the handling of tapes and discs must be clear.

Operational security is concerned with keeping files secure whilst the system is in operation and the files are being used. Common procedures and devices that can contribute to operational security are:

● *'Read-only' tabs* on floppy discs
● *Parity checks* on individual characters after they have been processed
● *Appropriate updating procedures*. It is important when updating a file to make sure that the new copy of the file does not overwrite the old copy. If the new file is corrupted, this will cause loss of the entire file. The new file should be written to temporary storage until the new copy has been checked as being correct
● *Grandfather-father-son* is an updating procedure which has tradition-ally been used with tapes. Tapes are often used as back-up storage, and this method ensures that adequate secure copies of files are maintained at all times. Three copies of each file are maintained which are described as the grandfather, father and son. Figure 5.2 demonstrates how the updating procedure operates

	Tape 1	Tape 2	Tape 3
Opening position	G	F*	S
1st update run	S ──────► G		F*
2nd update run	F*	S ──────► G	
3rd update run	G	F*	S

──► Direction of transfer
*Not used in update

Fig. 5.2 Updating procedure for file integrity

This procedure ensures that all copies are updated on a rational basis and that on each updating run the father tape is not involved in the updating process, so that it is immune from corruption.

Similar procedures can be adopted for files stored on other media such as discs

- *Dumping* file contents periodically to another medium such as from disc to tape ensures an additional and if necessary archival copy.
- *File labels* which are part of the recorded data can be used by the computer to check that the correct file has been set up, and may prevent unauthorized reading or writing.
- *Quantity and value totals* help to ensure that all records have been appropriately processed. For example, in adding a batch of order transactions it might be appropriate to calculate the total value of a batch of orders. This can be calculated both before and after input. If input is accurate and complete the two totals will tally.
- *Hash or nonsense totals* may be used in conjunction with quantity and value totals. For example, a nonsense total might be the total of the code numbers of items to be input, such as the total of ISBNs. By comparing this total for an input batch, prior to input and processing, with that after processing it is possible to check that all records have been processed.

Processing
Security during processing depends upon hardware and software reliability. Hardware errors such as non-functioning of hardware components are generally detected by the hardware. They will arise from time to time but good choice of hardware will minimize their occurrence. Software errors can be minimized by thorough testing prior to implementation. A program trial log is valuable during testing. Thorough early operational checks are also important.

Output

Some standard checks to ensure that appropriate output is produced include:

- Always produce something from a planned output run, even if it is 'No details for this run' or 'No records retrieved for this search'
- Print a termination message at the end of output, e.g. 'End of report'
- Print control totals, to indicate that everything has been processed
- Print headings and page numbers, and possibly the date and time on each page.

Once print-out has been produced efforts are needed to control the print-out. Records of its location, recipients' confidentiality levels, and number of copies need to be kept.

Systems review and evaluation

There are two basic kinds of systems review: immediate review of the system to check that it is working satisfactorily, and on-going longer-term systems evaluation to check that the system remains appropriate for the organization in which it is operating. Both types of review are likely to lead to the need to amend the existing system through appropriate maintenance procedures.

Initial systems review

The initial systems review should be regarded as the final stage of implementation. A system has not been successfully implemented until a satisfactory systems review has been conducted. On the other hand, the systems review should not be used as an excuse for prolonging the implementation phase. It is therefore important that the systems review takes place shortly after the full system (or if appropriate identifiable parts of it) is fully implemented. The system must have been operating for a sufficient period for all system processes to have been performed and to be working at full volume. Any recommendations for change arising from the systems review should be promptly considered by management and changes introduced as soon as possible.

The initial systems review should be conducted by someone qualified to do so, such as a systems analyst, but, clearly, in the interests of objectivity, not the same person as was responsible for the design and implementation of the system.

The initial review should assess whether the system meets its objectives, as outlined in the user's requirements specification. Major topics for consideration can be divided into system requirements and system performance.

1 *The system requirements* will be outlined in the original user's requirements specification and possibly modified later during the development of the system. The system needs to be evaluated against an up-to-date version of the systems requirements. An evaluation of how well the system meets its requirements must ensure that the system satisfactorily fulfils all of its objectives. Clearly, a system can be expected to meet most of the system objectives; careful attention needs to be paid to those areas where it is not completely successful.

Matters which are likely to be subject to review are:

- The cost of the system, both in terms of initial start-up costs, and in terms of running costs
- Whether the system makes the appropriate processes easier, quicker or more efficient
- Whether any additional processes or data that the system was required to generate are provided in an appropriate form, and found to be useful.

More specific aspects of the system requirements may be assessed by examining the performance of the system.

2 *Performance* should be evaluated both objectively and subjectively. A primary concern during performance evaluation is to ascertain user response to the system. Once the system is fully operational users are likely to be in a position to refine, in various minor respects, their expectations of it. Problems may arise with:

- The nature and extent of reports produced by the system
- The interface between the system and manual procedures
- Any run schedules associated with batch updating files
- Computer procedures may deviate from those in documented instruction
- Arrangements for privacy and security may need to be reviewed
- System-response times need to be checked, especially if the system is more heavily used than predicted
- Error levels settle to an acceptable level
- System-use levels must be assessed and compared with predicted levels
- Any environmental changes in the system since implementation need to be monitored.

System maintenance

System maintenance involves the correction of faults and the enhancement of system functions. Requests for system maintenance may arise from:

- A review of a recently implemented system
- An audit of a long-standing system
- Ad hoc user requests for system improvements
- Changes in system requirements resulting from environmental changes.

System maintenance accounts for a significant proportion of the cost of the entire system. It is therefore important that system maintenance be effective and efficient.

The organization must establish procedures for system amendment. Each requested amendment must go through established channels and be fully discussed before being implemented. All implications must be fully explored and discussed, and any changes fully documented.

Amendment and maintenance procedures should:

(a) Allow any member of staff to request an amendment.
(b) Ensure that all amendments are suitably authorized. There must be some central control over amendments.
(c) Full documentation of systems faults should be available before a decision is made to proceed with an amendment.
(d) Documentation must be updated to take account of any amendments.
(e) Some form of priority grading must be agreed so that work programmes can be planned. Priority will depend on the effect of the amendment on system objectives, system costs, other systems, users and data security, as well as the workload of any staff involved in effecting the amendment.

Amendments will vary significantly in size. Amendments may affect any aspect of the system from the human—computer interface through clerical procedures to documentation. Major amendments need to be treated as small-scale development projects, and need to go through most of the same phases as a full systems-analysis-and-design exercise.

A system will continue to be maintained until it no longer reflects the objectives of the organization and it becomes appropriate to investigate the need for a new system.

Longer-term systems evaluation

All systems need to be subject to a periodic review procedure. Reviews may be conducted on an annual basis, or less frequently. The objective of such a procedure is to monitor the extent to which a system is still fulfilling its objectives. Many of the topics which form the subject of an initial systems review also need to be re-examined during the periodic review process.

Systems decay

The periodic review process is likely to reveal changes in:

- Systems requirements
- Systems environment

and ageing of:

- Hardware
- Software
- Telecommunications.

Eventually, a time will come when the costs of maintaining a system to take account of any of these factors will not justify the benefit. Alternatively, the software and/or hardware market will change so that new options become available for, say, networks or data input, which were not available during the initial systems design. When it becomes evident that a completely new system might offer significant additional benefits, the time has come to complete the system life-cycle and to start a new systems-analysis project.

Further reading

Barron, R., 'Automating Devon', *Library Association record*, **90** (3), March 1988, 150.

Boss, R. W., *The library manager's guide to automation*, 2nd ed., White Plains (NY), Knowledge Industry Publications, 1984.

Burton, P. F. and Petrie, J. H., *The librarian's guide to microcomputers for information management*, Wokingham, Van Nostrand Reinhold, 1986.

Chapman, E. A. and others, *Library systems analysis guidelines*, New York and London, Wiley-Interscience, 1970.

Corbin, J. B., *Developing computer-based library systems*, 2nd ed., Phoenix (Arizona), Oryx Press, 1985.

Davis, W. S., *Tools and techniques for structured systems analysis and design*, London, Addison-Wesley, 1983.

Eastlake, J. J., *A structured approach to computer strategy*, Chichester Ellis Horwood, 1987.

Farrow, H. F., *Computerisation guidelines*, Manchester, National Computing Centre, 1980.

Francis, S., 'Management problems arising from the introduction of automation', *The electronic library journal*, 1984, 25−30.

Gates, H., 'Factors to consider in choosing a microcomputer for library housekeeping and information retrieval in a small library', *Program*, **18**, April 1984, 111−23.

Gosling, J., *SWALCAP: a guide for librarians and systems managers*, Aldershot, Gower, 1987.

Lancaster, F. W., 'Systems analysis and design for libraries', *Library trends*, **21**, 1973, 463–612.

Library Association, *The impact of new technology on library and information centres*, London, LA, 1983.

Matthews, J. R., *Choosing an automated library system: a planning guide*, Chicago, American Library Association, 1980.

Matthews, J. R., *A reader on choosing an automated library system*, Chicago, American Library Association, 1983.

National Computing Centre, *Systems training*, Manchester, National Computing Centre, 1984.

Revill, D. and Cowley, J., *Working papers on automation*, Oxford, Council of Polytechnic Librarians, 1985.

Rowbottom, M., 'First steps in choosing information retrieval packages', *Library micromation news*, April 1984, 13–16.

Rowbottom, M. and Templeton, R., 'Getting started – a guide to using the microcomputer in the library', *Library micromation news*, special issue, 1985.

Townley, H. M., *Systems analysis for information retrieval*, London, Andre Deutsch, 1978.

Trevelyan, A. and Rowat, M., *Systems programs in library applications of microcomputers*, London, British Library, 1983 (Library and Information Research Report, No. 12).

Wainwright, J., 'Negotiating for a contract – drawing up the technical specification', *Program*, **13** (4), October 1979, 158–64.

Westlake, D. R. and Clarke, J. E., *GEAC: a guide for librarians and systems managers*, Aldershot, Gower, 1987.

Index

Notes In order to avoid a long list of terms under 'systems', topics are generally not listed under 'systems' if there is a satisfactory alternative. So, for example, 'Systems methodologies' is indexed under 'Methodologies' and 'Systems users' is indexed under 'Users'.
Filing order is word-by-word.